forgotten
TALES
of
MISSOURI

forgotten TALES of MISSOURI

Mary Collins Barile

illustrations by

Karleigh Hambrick

THE
History
PRESS

Published by The History Press
Charleston, SC 29403
www.historypress.net

First published 2012

Manufactured in the United States

ISBN 978.1.60949.473.5

Library of Congress CIP data applied for.

CONTENTS

Preface

*Tale: A story told to interest or amuse
or to record the history of fact or fiction.*

*Legend: A story thought to be historical,
but not verifiable; a mixture of fact and fiction.*

Tales and legends are the perfect literary form for
Missouri; so many stories there are bigger than life
and have shaped the image of the American West yet are
difficult to pin down with facts. Trying to tame a Missouri
legend onto the page is like trying to lasso a bear: you start
out with confidence, rope the critter and then realize there
is nothing much you can do but hang on and follow the tale
to its lair, hoping for the best.

In every Missouri legend is a clue to who Missourians are
and who they were. Track back the history of a legend and
a reader can often spy remnants of earlier stories. Missouri

was settled thousands of years ago from the north and northwest by people who became the Osage, Kaw, Sauk and Fox and later by Europeans who brought with them their stories of old, of gods, ancestor heroes, ghosts and mischief makers. It is a measure of the strength of legends and tales that old and new coexist comfortably.

Old stories took root over generations. Today, the Internet can create legends overnight, but still the idea remains strong: a person or place or animal, a nub of truth and a web of lies, a blend of hope, humor and mystery. For the most part, the stories included in this book have been tracked back to earlier tales, not to deny the truth, but only to examine it more closely.

Truth, after all, still remains stranger and more engaging than most legends. And Missouri, of course, leads every other place in truth.

Or so they say.

Acknowledgements

Every word in every book is inspired by people and memories, and I am grateful to my friends for their support and help. I wish especially to thank the following people for being there despite my obsession with these stories: Margaret Barile, Janet Acton, Sara Arrandale, Elinor Barrett, Susan Meadows and Karen Neely, James Cogswell, Deb Entwistle, Susan Flader, Arlene Hoose, Brett Johnson, Christine Montgomery, Richard Wallace, Laura Vollmer and everyone at Never the Same.

As always, the staff at The History Press have made this project a happy romp through the past. Thanks again to editor Ben Gibson for reminding me why writing is fun.

I would also like to acknowledge that historians receive as much help from the dead as they do from the living and that to explore another's life is an honor. So thank you to all those folks whose stories appear in this book—it was a pleasure meeting you.

Chapter 1

Missouri's Fault

Dear Sir,
In compliance with your request, I will now give you a history,
as full in detail as the limits of the letter will permit, of the
late awful visitation of Providence in this place and vicinity.
On the 16th of December, 1811, about two o'clock,
A.M., we were visited by a violent shock of an earthquake,
accompanied by a very awful noise resembling loud but distant
thunder, but more hoarse and vibrating, which was followed
in a few minutes by the complete saturation of the atmosphere,
with sulphurious vapor, causing total darkness. The screams
of the affrighted inhabitants running to and fro, not knowing
where to go, or what to do—the cries of the fowls and beasts
of every species—the cracking of trees falling, and the roaring
of the Mississippi—the current of which was retrograde for a
few minutes, owing as is supposed, to an irruption in its bed—
formed a scene truly horrible.
—excerpt from a letter, Eliza Bryant to Lorenzo Dow

Eliza Bryant lived near the village of New Madrid along the Mississippi River in southern Missouri when the earth started to heave and twist to the dance of geologic plates deep underground. For her friends and neighbors, the reason behind the terror was hardly the point, as they grabbed what they could and tried to find higher ground in the dark and confusion. Bryant survived the destruction of her village and the surrounding landscape and lived in New Madrid for the rest of her life (she died in 1866 at the age of eighty-six), leaving behind one of the most riveting descriptions of Missouri during what one contemporary called "a time of extraordinaries." The quakes reached between 7 and 8 or higher on the Richter scale and extended over more than one million square miles. Reports said shaking was felt as far east as Pennsylvania and Washington, D.C., where First Lady Dolley Madison awoke one morning to the temblors. The initial quake occurred in Arkansas on December 16, the second in Missouri near the Bootheel on January 23 and the final great quake on the land between Missouri and Tennessee on February 7, 1812. There may have been more than two thousand aftershocks, which rattled land and nerves daily for more than a year, but the quakes haunted those who survived throughout their lives.

The horrors of the events were nearly indescribable, although many people tried to do just that. Settlers and Native Americans experienced land tremors, landslides, rifts and sand blows that sent coal, mud, water and debris shooting into the air with great force. One sand blow—formed when the land was saturated with water—covered more than one hundred acres and is still visible on the New Madrid landscape. During the quakes, the earth was literally torn apart and fissures split the land. Several stories were told of men who escaped by leaping onto trees and sitting astride them above the fissures until the earth stopped shaking. A Native American camp was swallowed up, with only one man escaping by climbing out of a crater. He believed that the quake had been foretold by the Prophet, a Shawnee religious leader and shaman and brother of the great Tecumseh. Father Joseph, a priest, was on a boat bound from St. Louis to New Orleans and wrote of the first quake, "It was dark. We saw two houses on fire on the left bank and when we came to New Madrid there were houses also burning there. The people were crowded out upon the hillside and were in great fear." Reports of booming thunder and lightning flashes from the earth may have occurred as quartz crystals were squeezed with enough force to produce heat and sparks of light on the surface. (The cause of seismo-luminescence, or earthquake lights, is still unknown and has been attributed to chemicals, heat and electrical buildup from the quakes.)

Newspapers and writers saw quakes as a test for Missourians who were viewed as rough and ready and somewhat irreligious. (The Baptist missionary John Mason Peck was told by Missourians that the Sabbath never crossed the Mississippi.) One writer from North Carolina was pleased with the effects of the quake, noting, "A wonderful change has taken place in the manners of the people. I believe so many fervent prayers never were put up in this place as on that fearful night and morning. I hope what has been done may produce a revival in religion." Others treated the New Madrid quakes with somewhat greater awe and less gloating, as did this poem from the *Baptist Missionary Magazine*, published on March, 1812:

> *Still was the hour. The Moon drove high*
> *Her cloudless course along the sky.*
> *The winds were hush'd; no zephyr's sigh*
> *Breath'd o'er the deep tranquillity.*
> *What awful stillness reigns around;*
> *Nature seems sunk in sleep profound.*
> *What sudden trembling moves the ground!*
> *What shakes the earth so fearfully?*
> *Earth's bosom seems with pain to swell.*
> *What wand'ring spirit strikes that bell!*
> *Nature, is this thy funeral knell?*
> *My soul, is this eternity?*
> *How dread the Earthquake's awful roll,*
> *That shakes the earth from pole to pole!*
> *What power can thus convulse the whole?*
> *Can it be less than Deity?*

Colonel John Shaw of Wisconsin was visiting near New Madrid just before the February 7, 1812 shock. He and scores of other people fled from their houses up and down the river and headed to Tywappity (or Zawapita, perhaps a tangled version of the Spanish word for "pretty") Hill, which stood back from the river. Shaw recalled:

> *This was the first high ground above New Madrid, and here the fugitives formed an encampment. It was proposed that all should kneel and engage in supplicating God's mercy, and all simultaneously. Catholics and Protestants, knelt and offered solemn prayer to their Creator. About twelve miles back toward New Madrid a young woman about seventeen years of age, named Betsy Masters, had been left by her parents and family, her right leg having been broken below the knee by the falling of one of the weight poles of the roof of the cabin, and, though a total stranger, I was the only person who would consent to return and see whether she still survived. Receiving a description of the locality of the place, I started and found the poor girl upon a bed as she had been left, with some water and cornbread within her reach. I cooked up some food for her and made her condition as comfortable as circumstances would allow and returned the same day to the grand encampment. Miss Masters eventually recovered.*

Other stories told of people with broken legs and arms who, despite the unsanitary conditions, managed to avoid losing their limbs and survived the earthquakes. But despite all the narratives recalling how the land writhed and split, perhaps the most frightening place to be during the quakes was not near but on the Mississippi River. Eliza Bryan recalled seeing something that must have appeared as the end of the world:

> At first the Mississippi seemed to recede from its banks, and its waters gathering up like a mountain, leaving for the moment many boats on bare sand, in which time the poor sailors made their escape from them. It then rising fifteen to twenty feet perpendicularly, and expanding, as it were, at the same moment, the banks were overflowed with the retrograde current, rapid as a torrent—the boats which before had been left on the sand were now torn from their moorings, and suddenly driven up a little creek, at the mouth of which they laid, to the distance in some instances, of nearly a quarter of a mile. The river falling immediately, as rapid as it had risen, receded in its banks again with such violence, that it took with it whole groves of young cotton-wood trees, which ledged its borders. They were broken off which such regularity, in some instances, that persons who had not witnessed the fact, would be difficultly persuaded, that it has not been the work of art. A great many fish were left on the banks, being unable to keep pace with the water. The river was literally covered with the wrecks of boats, and 'tis said that one was wrecked in which there was a lady and six children, all of whom were lost.

The river ran backward as the quake forced up the riverbed and blocked the current, and new rapids threatened any boat that survived swamping. The number of Missourians killed during the quakes is unknown, but many boatmen and river travelers must have perished under the waves. Among the most personal of the recollections of the great Missouri quakes was one left by John Wiseman, a boatman who was some miles below New Madrid and who, despite his experiences, returned to Missouri to live after the quakes ceased:

> *I was awakened by the roaring noise and if my flatboat load of whiskey had sprung a leak and made the "Father of Waters" drunk it could not have committed more somersaults. It seemed that old Vesuvius himself was drunk, and from that time on, at intervals, that roaring and shaking of the earth continued until the 7th of February, and up to the 17th of February were many hard shakes, and on the latter day was one that excelled in noise, force, and terror all preceding ones, when the earth was rocked about like a cradle and its surface rolling like waves a few feet high and in places causing fissures in the earth from which large volumes of warm water, sand and charcoal was blown up, the gas coming up from these fissures smelling like sulfur. The country immediately around where our boat was moored was not perceptibly sunk, but the country northwest and to the west from where came the roaring*

noise was sunk many feet. It was then that we saw a sandbar below us, that extended clear across the river, and the water commenced rolling in terrific waves up the current and broke our boat loose from her fastenings. This bar lasted only a short time; in a few hours the retrograde current soon spread over it again and we succeeded on making our boat fast with stout ropes and then abandoned it and returned on foot to New Madrid with two of my flat boat hands. On the way we crossed a bayou near whose bank was an "Indian wigwam" where lived [an] Indian chief name "Wapacapa" (John Big Knife). Seeing nothing of the chief we stepped to the door of his wigwam when he arose without any fear or terror depicted in his countenance, but with a hideous and woe-begon look, uttered "Woo! Hon Jo!!" (my friend,) and pointing his right hand finger to the heavens and with his left hand, showing the tottering motions of the earth, he said: "Great Spirit ke-chi-monito, whiskey too much: heap drunk, bine-by he make all gone Injun hunten ground." On our arrival at New Madrid we found all was destruction; the site of the town appeared to have sunk ten or twelve feet, we returned to our boat in a few days and found it secure whilst nearly all other boats were lost.

As the earth calmed down, people began to pick up what pieces remained of their lives and start again. Many refused to remain in the Mississippi River Valley and appealed to the government for assistance. William Clark, former explorer and now governor of the Missouri Territory, declared in January 1813:

> *Whereas, in the catalogue of miseries and afflictions, with which it has pleased the Supreme Being of the universe to visit the inhabitants of this earth are none more tragic and destructive than earthquakes—man's wisdom can not foresee nor his precaution guard against them. In whatever sections of the habitable world this wreck of matter, these convulsions of nature occur, they do not fail profoundly to impress us with awe and to express our astonishment at their terrible effects.*

Clark recognized that the loss of good farming land and homes would weaken future migration to the region, so he moved to ameliorate the disaster by encouraging people to remain in the Missouri Territory. "Many of these our unfortunate fellow citizens are now wandering about without a home to go to or a roof to shelter them from the pitiless storm." He reported that the General Assembly for the territory of Missouri, as well as the national legislature, would provide relief through money or land. New Madrid certificates were later issued for lands in Arkansas and Missouri, and although meant to help survivors, the certificates became the target of speculators and other ne'er-do-wells whose greed resulted in land title problems that lasted well into the early twentieth century.

Two centuries later, New Madrid waits today for the next major quake. While small tremors occur now and then, geologists disagree as to the chances for a major disaster, and but one thing is certain: if and when it occurs, so will the legends.

Chapter 2

LONG'S DRAGON

In the first decades of the nineteenth century, the United States expanded its boundaries, raised a government and worked to keep its borders secure. The War of 1812 had nearly cost the United States its hard-won independence, and the government was determined to maintain the safety of its people, lands and commerce. (Of course, the concerns and needs of Native Americans were hardly a part of this discussion.) The Louisiana Purchase lands had only just been explored by Meriwether Lewis, William Clark and the Corps of Discovery, and it was clear to the young country that encroachments by British fur trappers and traders would sow discord among local tribes and place at risk the profitable fur trade. The Rocky Mountains and the Great Plains might keep intrusions at bay for a time, but Missouri territory—rich in land, minerals and opportunity—still required security.

As part of the attempt to secure the western lands, in 1818, Secretary of War John Calhoun authorized the formation, provisioning and transportation of what became known as the Yellowstone Expedition, which consisted of three sections. Two military units were charged with constructing a series of forts up the Mississippi and Missouri Rivers and securing U.S. borderlands from Michigan to the Yellowstone River. The scientific mission—called the Scientific Expedition or the Long Expedition after the head engineer, Major Stephen Harriman Long—was charged with recording topographical, botanical and other data useful for future settlement, exploration and commerce. The expeditions were to organize in St. Louis and head north and west along the Mississippi and Missouri Rivers in 1819.

The troops arrived in St. Louis by early summer. Colonel Henry Atkinson commanded the First and Sixth Rifle Regiments, which traveled nearly 2,700 miles from the New York–Canada border to St. Louis. Stephen Long recruited scientists, journalists and artists to assist on the journey. Among them were zoologist and entomologist Thomas Say, botanist Edwin James (who was the first to ascend Pike's Peak), landscape artist Samuel Seymour and Titian Ramsey Peale, an artist and naturalist who was to collect insect and plant samples to preserve and sketch. (Some of Peale's collecting materials are held at the Museum of Westward Expansion in St. Louis.)

Public interest in the expeditions grew, perhaps because the soldiers and scientists did not travel in awkward, clunky keelboats but were propelled by a new power on the western waters: steam. The military constructed six steamboats to tackle the Missouri: the *Jefferson*, the *Expedition*, the *Johnson*, *Calhoun*, *Exchange* and the *Western Engineer*, the latter for the Long party. The *Engineer* was built in Pittsburgh, weighed thirty tons and drew less than two feet of water. The soldier/journalist Alphonso Wetmore, who was a member of the Yellowstone Expedition and later settled in Missouri, recalled his impressions on seeing this new method of western transportation:

> *Extending their walk to the river bank to look at "The Western Engineer," a steam boat which had been constructed for the special purpose of navigating the Missouri river, this small craft was observed just then getting under way. Marvelous as it might seem, some malconstruction of the machinery which was designed to propel the boat worked inversely, and carried her stern-foremost up stream…When the Western Engineer, the steamboat, which had run backwards, had been taught the Crocket system of "going ahead," the Missouri Expedition set forward, accompanied by this abortion of science and art…"They ain't got nothing to do now," said [a soldier], who was in attendance, "but to put the bowsprit on the stearn, and shift the rudder forward, and she will go like all nature."*

26

The boat left Pittsburgh on May 5 and arrived at St. Louis on June 9, having navigated rapids, low water and sandbars. By late June, the steamboats were working their way up the Missouri. The success rate of the military transports was abysmal: the *Calhoun* and the *Exchange* did not make it out of the Mississippi River, defeated by sand and grit that clogged their engines; the *Jefferson* gave up the ghost thirty miles or so below Franklin, Missouri; and while the *Expedition* and *Johnson* made it to Cow Island, near present-day Nebraska, the two ships had to return to St. Louis the next year and did not reach their goal of the Yellowstone River.

The *Missouri Gazette* on May 26, 1819, described the *Western Engineer* as well armed and "carries an elegant flag representing a white man and an Indian shaking hands, the calumet of peace and the sword. The board is 75 feet long, 13 feet beam and draws 19 inches of water." The ship was among the first stern-wheelers on the rivers and was equipped with mast and sails to be used if the steam failed. But the real curiosity was neither the steam nor the flag but the ship's construction, as revealed in a letter dated June 19, 1819:

> *The bow of this vessel exhibits the form of a huge serpent, black and scaly, rising out of the water from under the boat, his head as high as the deck, darted forward, his mouth open, vomiting smoke and apparently carrying the boat on his back. From under*

> *the boat at its stern issues a stream of foaming water,*
> *dashing violently along. All the machinery is hid.*
> *Three small brass field pieces mounted on the wheel*
> *carriages stand on the deck. The boat is ascending*
> *the rapid stream at the rate of three miles an hour.*
> *Neither wind nor human hands are seen to help her,*
> *and, to the eye of ignorance, the illusion is complete,*
> *that a monster of the deep carries her on his back,*
> *smoking with fatigue, and lashing the waves with*
> *violent exertion.*

The ship was nicknamed "Long's Dragon," and its design was meant to shock and awe viewers—especially Native Americans, who, it was believed, would flee the ghastly sight. In truth, a number of tribes were said to have laughed at the serpent, and some did not hesitate to visit the ship when invited by the commanders. Titian Ramsay Peale recalled that the ship appeared to be pulled along by the monster and that the sides of the wheel were marked "James Monroe" and "John C. Calhoun" because the president and secretary were "the propelling powers of the expedition."

The *Engineer* arrived at Franklin on July 13 and was greeted by more than one hundred people, a large crowd for a wilderness town. The crew and scientists stopped there for a week, where the men were fêted and celebrated at dinners and other events. (What the good people of Franklin did not yet realize was that the soldiers would eventually make the village a place for carousing, drinking and fighting, forcing Franklin to build a larger jail.)

After leaving Franklin, the *Western Engineer* chugged and steamed to Nebraska, where the ship wintered over after completing what many thought was an impossible task: ascending the Missouri River. The next spring, the ship was ordered back to St. Louis and later asked again for the impossible: the *Engineer* was sent up the Mississippi River to Keokuk in an effort to demonstrate that steam power would prove a conquering force in the American West. After its last journey, the *Western Engineer* disappeared from history, but it helped to launch the steamboat age and the dreams of Missourians for generations.

Chapter 3

THE CHAMBER POT WAR

The village of Cote sans Dessein (said to be pronounced in the old French as *Cote sans Dusaw*) was a French settlement begun around 1808 east of present-day Jefferson City. The "hill without design," which gave the village its name, was located near the mouth of the Osage River and was a prominent landmark, rising up along the Missouri River and stretching for more than a quarter mile. The hill appeared to be placed on the wrong side of the river, opposite other land elevations, but through changes in the river's flow from flooding or erosion, the hill was "captured" and separated from its fellows. The Cote sans Dessein settlement was a way station for traders and Native Americans, eventually growing to more than four hundred residents. The land was excellent for farming and described as having rich topsoil and "mould" more than four inches deep. But like many river settlements, in a few years the mad waters of the Missouri overcame the village, and the village was abandoned.

BATTLE OF COTE SANS
DESSEINS
° FOR MADAME ROI...
UR-INE-CREDIBLE!

According to T. Ferguson, who lived in the village in 1817, Cote sans Dessein had log houses and a blockhouse, or small fort, a blacksmith shop, a tavern and several small mercantile establishments. Only two years earlier, Cote sans Dessein had been the site of a battle between Fox and Sac Indians and settlers. Although the War of 1812 had officially ended in 1814, clashes between Indians and settlers still occurred on the frontier. On April 4,

1815, the Battle of Cote sans Desseins took place when a group of Sac and Fox attacked. The local militia fought most of the battle outside the village, but the blockhouse was cut off and surrounded. Inside, only a few men and a number of women and children attempted to hold off the attackers with rifle fire. The women reloaded the rifles, cast bullets and cut patches (the rifles were loaded with powder, a patch and a lead ball), and the blockhouse defenders held their own. Then the attack changed as the besiegers sent burning arrows onto the wooden roof. Several small fires were started but were extinguished by the women, using what little water they had on hand. But there is more to the legend than a heroic battle. Here is how a veteran of the War of 1812 told the story:

> *The principal actor in this achievement was a Frenchman, whose name was Baptiste Louis Roi. He chanced to be in the blockhouse, with only two men and as many women, when the attack commenced. With this small command he made a successful defence against a numerous and very determined band of Indians. The women, the wife and sister-in-law of the gallant Roi, lent efficient and indispensable aid to the two soldiers, their husbands. After the extreme suffering which the assailants endured, they became desperate in their determination to take or destroy the blockhouse and they determined to set fire to the house. To effect this in security, they fastened combustible matter to their*

arrows, and, having lighted this, their missives were shot into the roof of the block-house; as often as this occurred, the women made it a business to extinguish the blaze by the application of the little water they had within the building. The place of defence was near the river-bank, but the garrison was too weak to justify a sally for additional supplies. It was with appalling interest that the little band observed the rapid expenditure of their small stock as the incendiaries repeated their experiments. At last the water was exhausted, the last bucket was drained of the last drop! another discharge succeeded. The roof was blazing over their heads; and when despair was settling on the hitherto buoyant spirits of the little band, one of the females produced a gallon of milk. This was sufficient to protract destruction, but no security against a recurrence of imminent peril. There was a pause after the last blaze had been extinguished. The defenders were watching with acute sensibility every movement of the enemy, hoping that their fruitless efforts had discouraged them, and that in this they would win impunity. But when they began to respire freely with hope of safety, another discharge broke on their view; the fiery arrows hurled in the air, and the roof blazed again with fearful clearness! A mighty shout arose from a hundred wild and startling voices. Even Baptiste Roi himself, whose visage was the mirror of a hero's soul, looked aghast at the companions of his peril, until his wife, with an angel's smile upon her face, produced, from the urinal then replenished, the fluid that proved the salvation of the garrison. The fire was again extinguished. Thrice did these women supply from the same fountain the extinguishment of wicked hopes.

The story continued, noting that after the Missouri frontier achieved a lasting peace, several St. Louis gentlemen decided to present Baptiste Roi with a magnificent rifle to commemorate his victory. The men had also brought a present for Madame Roi, a silver urinal engraved with her name, to recall her role in the battle. Monsieur Roi was horrified and refused to accept either gift, tossing the gentlemen out of his house and the rifle and urinal after them. Today, the hill of Cote sans Dessein is still visible, but nothing remains of the village except the legend of a battle won by piss and vinegar.

Chapter 4

Mike Fink in Missouri

The most colorful characters to stride through early Missouri river towns were the keelboatmen, a hard-driving, profane band of brothers who held the river under their sway while sober and even more so when drunk. Although their hijinks were recalled with nostalgia, few of their names outlasted their antics, except for one: Mike Fink. The toughest man on American rivers, Fink is still associated with the Ohio in its heyday as a liquid highway, but he left his mark on Missouri as well, and that is a legend rarely told.

Keelboats were the workhorses of the great western waters. Large, up to eighty feet or more, the boats had a slight keel, pointed ends (unlike a flat-edged raft) and could be powered by sail, pole, oar or hand-over-hand. In fact, "to bushwhack" in earlier times meant to pull a boat upstream by using brute strength, grabbing branches and bushes to haul the vessel against the current. Perhaps the most famous keelboats were those used by Lewis and Clark's Corps of Discovery on their way to the Pacific Ocean. Keelboats were used for exploration, military troop transport and cargo, following the Alleghany, Ohio and Mississippi Rivers to St. Louis, Cairo and New Orleans, and the men who were attracted to the shipping business needed to be tough, brave and foolhardy. No one suited that description better than Mike Fink.

Fink's birth date is unknown, but he was born around the year 1770 in Fort Pitt, Pennsylvania, near the Monongahela River. The settlement was rough and primitive, a dangerous place to grow up. It was under constant threat of attack by Native Americans, and there was little time for youthful frolics. Stories contemporary with Fink seem to indicate that he wanted to be a keelboatman from childhood and that he was famous for imitating the sound of the boatman's horn and all its tunes.

By the time Fink was a teenager, he had served as a scout for the military and was an unparalleled shot with a rifle, no mean reputation in a land where men and women could load, aim and fire a black powder weapon in seconds. Fink was described as five feet, nine inches, 180 pounds, with a "broad round face, pleasant features, brown skin tanned by sun and rain; blue, but very expressive eyes, inclining to grey, broad white teeth, and square brawny form." He was a physically powerful man and was generally the winner of every fight. His reputation began to attract stories about his life and skills, but such tales

were also racist and mean-spirited, reflecting the fears and prejudices of earlier times. Fink once shot the tails off a family of pigs from a great distance, leaving the poor animals frightened but otherwise unharmed. Fink's wife was also the butt of his jokes, although she apparently had faith in his skills, as described by a distant relative:

> In the management of his business Mike Fink was a rigid disciplinarian: woe to the man who shirked his responsibilities or did not carry his own weight— literally. He always had his woman along with him, and would allow no other man to speak with her. She was sometimes a subject for his wonderful skill in marksmanship with the rifle. He would have her hold on the top of her head a tin cup filled with whiskey, which he would put a bullet through. Another of his feats was to have her hold it between her knees, as in a vise, and then shoot.

Fink was such an outstanding shot that he was barred from contests. But he was not a man to trifle with; he struck a deal that if he was to stop competing, he was to receive the hide and tallow of the beef, which he then traded to the local tavern owner in exchange for drinks to entertain his friends and fellow boatmen. Tough he may have been, but Fink was also fair, giving bonuses to those men who worked hard on his keelboat, making him an unusual boss among boatmen. He would proclaim, "I am a salt river roarer, and I love the wimming and I'm chock full of fight." Timothy Flint, a missionary who traveled and lived in Missouri, said that Mike had "a chère amie in every port…and always had a circle of worshippers around him, who would fight to their deaths for him." No village wanted to cross the boatmen, since their idea of entertainment consisted of stretching a rope across a street with several other "keelers" on each end. At a signal, the men would run down the street, tossing everyone and everything into the air.

Fink visited St. Louis as early as 1814 or '15, when he was in his mid-forties. By 1822, Mike had joined the Henry and Ashley fur-trapping company from St. Louis and traveled up the Missouri to the Yellowstone River, where the men set up camp for trapping. Fink was such a colorful character that he attracted the attention of Alphonso Wetmore, who wrote the first theatrical play west of the Mississippi. Wetmore, a military officer posted to St. Louis and Franklin, Missouri, had traveled to Pittsburgh, as well as the upper Missouri, and was familiar with many of the men who worked the river. It is very possible that Wetmore either met Fink or saw him in person; at the very least, Wetmore was familiar with the stories of Fink and his shenanigans in the river towns.

In *The Pedlar*, which was produced in St. Louis during the spring of 1821, the Mike Fink character makes his entrance "a little drunk" and later boasts, "I wouldn't give one glass of this old Monongahela for all the Madeira slops in Philadelphia." Fink calls himself a snapping turtle, a wildcat and "a steam boat, damn your eyes. I'm a snag, a five-horse team, a Missouri snag, I'm into you." His costume consisted of a "glazed leather hat, red flannel shirt, linen overalls," common dress for a Missouri boatman. *The Pedlar* showed that Mike Fink was a local figure in Missouri and part of the state's culture.

Although Fink was depicted as larger-than-life, Mike's story did not come with a happy ending. During the winter of 1822, Mike and two friends—Talbot and Carpenter—lived in a cave with other boatmen to escape the brutal storms. Mike and his friends were all crack shots; they would "sky a copper" (toss a coin into the air) and shoot it right through the center. But their favorite show of skill was knocking a mug of whiskey off each other's heads from a distance. During the winter, Mike and Carpenter quarreled, but it wasn't until later that year that the argument turned deadly, and Mike shot Carpenter during the mug trick. Mike first swore that it was an accident, and no one dared to dispute it. But later that year, in his cups, Mike confessed to Talbot that he had murdered Carpenter. Without a second's hesitation, Talbot drew out his pistol and shot Mike Fink dead. No one knows where Fink is buried, but the Missouri River still echoes with his boat horn and his stories.

Chapter 5

THE VICTORIA WITCH

In 1802, Georgia native Thomas L. Bevis pushed his way through brush and brier to settle a tract of land in the Missouri mineral district, near present-day Victoria. The land contained rich deposits of lead, iron, copper, zinc and clay and provided families with mining and farming opportunities. Besides the wealth beneath the soil, the region above offered the natural beauty of bluffs, rivers, crystal-clear streams and deep forest. Bevis came into a land that was unsettled and relatively unexplored by white emigrants. He may have moved into the district to take advantage of the Spanish government's offer of free land to those who would homestead. (Bevis knew Daniel Boone, who three years earlier had moved near present-day Marthasville to take advantage of the same offer.)

Thomas Bevis was born in 1750, and little is known of his life before Missouri. He married Polly Herod in Missouri, and they had at least one child, but Polly later left Bevis's bed and board and moved on. Bevis formalized the break in August 1808, when he placed a notice in the St. Louis *Missouri Gazette* saying that he was no longer responsible for Polly's care or debts. He later lived with Prudence Childers Mars (or Maurs), and they had five children. Mars family lore said that Prudence was Irish and Cherokee and from a very large family who lived in Missouri. Bevis farmed and worked for some time as a blacksmith, and his landholdings were confirmed in 1810: he received about one hundred acres of land, the bounty allowed to single men. Apparently first unable to prove the legitimacy of his marriage and his children, he was later given the full bounty of more than five hundred acres due to a husband and father. Bevis died in 1826, survived by his wife and six children, since Prudence cared for her stepdaughter as well. Their children were still living in Missouri as late as 1912. (One of his daughters was struck and killed by that smoking emblem of progress, a train.) A monument to his intrepidness in defying the wilderness was raised to him in 1904 near Victoria. But Bevis did not leave a simple, mourning family as part of his contribution to society. He, in fact, left behind a widow who would become the terror of the region—for Prudence Childers Mars Bevis was a witch.

Witchcraft in Missouri has a long history, less known than the tales of New Orleans and Salem but just as serious when it came to witches and community reaction. Both native peoples and white settlers held common ideas about witchcraft: that a witch could curse or conjure or place a spell on an enemy, and that curse could only be removed by the action of a skilled witch doctor. In 1805, the death of a Lenape chief in Indiana (possibly from smallpox) resulted in rumors that he was murdered by witchcraft. Tenskwatawa—called the Prophet—was the brother of the Indian leader Tecumseh. The Prophet encouraged witch hunts among the Delaware, Shawnee and other tribes, binding the fear of white incursion and Christianity to the loss of native lands and culture. He accused native people who were friendly to whites of witchcraft, and in a terrible echo of Salem, men and women accused of sorcery and magic were tried by the Prophet and then turned over to his followers for execution.

The hysteria spread in 1809 to Missouri, where Shawnee and Delaware tribal members executed several dozen Indians after accusing them of causing epidemics and turning themselves into animals at will. Tecumseh traveled to the Shawnee village near Cape Girardeau and was able to end the slaughter through reason and negotiation. White settlements in the area feared attacks by the witch hunters, and the episode remained clear in the memory of settlers for many years.

But the belief in witchcraft did not originate with native peoples, as white immigrants brought with them traditions from the old country. Vance Randolph, folklorist and writer, lived and worked in the Missouri and Arkansas Ozark region for decades. As late as the

1940s, he recorded many witchcraft beliefs that were still strong in the region. Missouri tradition told of horsehair sieves (nets) placed over windows or cracks in doorways, the belief being that a witch had to go in and out of each hole and, therefore, would be distracted from entering the cabin. A witch might pledge to serve the Devil and, in return, gain power to cause illness, ruin crops and hasten death or other tragedies. One Ozark tradition was that for a woman to become a true witch, someone else had to die: "the witch's pence." In a time of poor sanitation and diseases like malaria, dysentery and cholera, the chance was great of someone dying without much warning, so a witch did not have to look far for her pence. She could also be a woman who used herbs and incantations to tell the future, find lost items or care for illness. But in many cases, when a woman was believed to be a witch, that alone was enough for her to be shunned by the community.

Prudence Bevis was the perfect example of a Missouri witch. More than thirty years younger than Thomas, she was described as a fine-looking woman with an independent spirit. Upon her husband's death, Prudence was unable to prove the legitimacy of her marriage—a costly problem, as Prudence found out, since it would be Thomas's first wife and daughter who inherited his estate. So, despite her contributions to settlement, Prudence was an outcast from the community in law, if not in spirit. Prudence raised Thomas's daughter, Rebecca, from his first marriage, and the couple had five children of their own: four before Thomas's death and one after. Thomas may have indeed been the father of all, but a birth after a husband's death could be easily twisted by gossip to appear to represent something other than undying devotion. Prudence's mixed heritage was also suspect: both the Irish and Indians had beliefs deeply rooted in ancient cultures, which did not often mesh well with the more conservative settlers and missionaries.

After Thomas's death, rumors of his widow's powers began to circulate. She was now "Queen Bevis" or "Queen Bevers" to the local people, who feared her influence. The reason for her title is lost, but she certainly ruled the imaginations of locals. Whenever illness, accident or bad luck befell someone, it was blamed on Prudence. One man complained that he could not aim at and shoot a deer; surely Queen Bevis was the reason. The hunter called in Henry H. Jones, a witch master. (The man or woman who could turn back a witch's wrath and spells upon her was called a witch master, a witch doctor, a conjure man or a white witch.) To un-bewitch the rifle, Jones drew a picture of Prudence and then fired a silver ball into the paper. Soon after, Prudence was seen hobbling around her garden with a bandaged leg, and the hunter got his deer. Another time, Prudence asked to purchase a cow from her neighbor, who refused the offer. The next day, the cow jumped the fence and ran off. When it was found days later, it gave bloody milk and was never useful again, a fact laid at the feet of Queen Bevis. Worse, Prudence was accused of causing illness in a neighbor's child. The little girl had an infection, and when a witch doctor removed a "hairball" from the wound, the child recovered. Perhaps the most famous accusation leveled against Prudence came from a farmer named Aaron Cook, who lived near Hillsboro, the county seat of Jefferson County, Missouri. Aaron claimed that Prudence turned him into a horse and rode him over hill and dale to a dance at Meridith Wideman's farm. Cook also charged that he was left outside the house and tied to a plum bush all night until Prudence returned him home, wet, tired and miserable.

Prudence was aware of her reputation but remained seemingly good-natured about it throughout her life, laughing away the reports of her activities. She must have had a fine sense of humor, since records appear to indicate that she leased land to a campground for religious revival meetings next to her farm. In later years, her reputation as a witch declined, and she moved to St. Louis, where she died around 1859, not the last of her kind in Missouri but certainly among the most colorful.

Chapter 6

Old Sawbones

Dr. Joseph Nash McDowell

Missouri certainly had its share of eccentrics and oddballs, men and women who stood out from the crowds of immigrants and settlers. But few could compete with Dr. Joseph Nash McDowell, a brilliant, bizarre and vituperative medical doctor who helped institute the study of medicine in Missouri and, in the act, inspired Mark Twain.

Joseph McDowell was born on April 1, 1805, in Kentucky to a family who contributed much to American medicine. Joseph studied with his uncle Ephraim McDowell, one of the earliest surgeons to practice on the frontier and a medical visionary. While boarding with Ephraim, Joseph fell in love with his cousin, but she rejected his proposal. In an early display of his temper, Joseph blamed his uncle for interfering in the romance and left the McDowell household, never to return.

Joseph McDowell eventually received a medical degree from Transylvania University in Kentucky and served as the chairman of the school's anatomy department. While in Kentucky, McDowell made a study of how disease affected the body and developed ideas about treatment. He theorized that because mountain air seemed to help European tuberculosis patients, perhaps cold cave air might benefit patients as well, and he established a small hospital within Kentucky's Mammoth Cave to test this hypothesis. (Never a shrinking violet, McDowell carved his name and the year, 1839, on the Giant's Coffin, a large rock within the cave system. The signature can still be seen.) Eventually, McDowell became a leading anatomist, as well as a popular teacher. He worked in Cincinnati and Pennsylvania, married, had children and finally made his way to St. Louis, where he settled for the rest of his life.

In 1840, McDowell founded the medical department of Kemper College (St. Louis), later known as the Missouri Medical College or McDowell's Medical College and associated for a short time with the young University of Missouri. In keeping with his love of learning and the bizarre, McDowell opened a museum of curiosities, containing examples of natural history exhibits, medical displays and other attractions, which became one of the most popular tourist stops in St. Louis. McDowell himself suited the museum's oddities. He was described in a contemporary medical journal as *very thin and much about the general height. His face was thin, features sharp, with high cheek bones and small piercing black eyes which seemed to look into the very recesses of one's soul. He early became known as "saw bones," which pseudonym he bore through life. He was a very profane man, not hesitating to speak his mind either in or out of the operating room. He was devoted to his friends and an eternal enemy to those he did not like. He was a fine anatomist, and is said to have amputated more arms and legs than any other man in St. Louis.*

McDowell spoke in an extremely high voice and was eccentric to the point of lunacy, dressing in a Continental soldier's uniform on holidays and firing off the school cannon, to the horror of his neighbors. He hated Catholics, interracial marriage and abolitionists, yet as far as is known, he never refused to treat a patient based on his personal beliefs. He lectured his students against drinking as he sipped gin and expected that his class would escort him home when he was drunk. He was terrified of thunderstorms and would crawl under a table or bed for protection. When spiritualism was taking root in America, McDowell explored the world of séances and mediums with an open mind. He used "lurid" language and, as one colleague said, was viewed by his neighbors— among them Jesuit priests—as a "vice regnant deputy of His Satanic Majesty."

Dr. McDowell was a popular instructor respected for his stories and his knowledge of anatomy. He taught during a time when medical students could graduate solely through reading texts and attending lectures, without having touched a living patient or even a cadaver. McDowell disagreed with that tradition and made certain that both he and his students studied the human body in—so to speak—the flesh. In order to do so, McDowell added another line to his résumé: resurrectionist. A healer by day, he turned grave robber and body snatcher by night. The need for bodies in research was desperate: St. Louis had a law allowing unclaimed bodies to be sent to medical schools, but the distribution system was based on the number of medical students per school and did not provide cadavers according to class needs. This gap forced legitimate, trained doctors to pay for the privilege of advancing their profession and improving medical care. Grave robbing was detested by the public but was extremely common, especially in cities. As St. Louis grew in size, cemeteries were moved to accommodate the expansion. Workers at the cemeteries could make extra money providing bodies to the colleges, and often when coffins were disinterred, it was discovered that wood and rocks weighted down the box—the body had been taken earlier. Despite the public's queasiness about body snatching, stealing a body was only a misdemeanor; it turned into a felony only if one stole the coffin or personal goods from the corpse.

McDowell took matters into his own hands: he led his students on grave-robbing forays into local cemeteries and located bodies that showed the effects of unusual diseases or conditions. The grave robbing was not without macabre humor: one time, a corpse sat up and pointed a pistol at McDowell, but this turned out to be a student joke. Another time, McDowell was nearly shot by angry locals when he acquired the body of a young girl from a resurrectionist. McDowell was in the dissecting room when a crowd broke into the college in search of the cadaver and the doctor. He managed to carry the body upstairs and hide it in the attic, but as he was coming down the staircase to escape, he realized he was trapped by the mob. According to his story, McDowell saw the ghost of his mother appear in front of him and motion to one of the dissecting tables. The doctor immediately climbed onto the table and covered himself with a sheet. In seconds, the crowd surged in and searched the room, but wary of the bodies, they only glanced at the "corpses" before continuing on their way. McDowell later told his students that he often thanked his mother's spirit for her quick thinking.

Although McDowell's College had an outstanding reputation based on the doctor's skills, he had competition for students as well as for corpses. The St. Louis University medical department, a Jesuit institution also known as Pope's College after the founder, Charles Pope, was attracting many students to its halls. A staunch Catholic, Pope was also the son-in-law of John O'Fallon, a wealthy and influential St. Louisan and represented much of what McDowell detested. McDowell took it into his head that members of Pope's College wanted to kill him in revenge for his opposition, so for years he wore a brass breastplate over his clothing and carried weapons. His own college was built and armed like a fortress. At one point in his younger days, McDowell had hoped to attack and capture upper California, and so inspired, he purchased 1,400 used muskets from the government and had a brass cannon built and installed on the ramparts of the school. Despite all this, McDowell was content to work with another St. Louis Medical College doctor, William McPheeters, as staff physician for the United States Marine Hospital for sick and disabled river boatmen, another indication of the doctor's ability to separate personal beliefs from medical treatment.

But of all his eccentricities, McDowell remains best known for his Missouri cave experiment. In 1840, McDowell purchased a cave just outside of Hannibal and blocked it off with a heavy gate. One of his plans was to "maintain" his family, friends and faculty members after death in a mausoleum at the medical school, and he spent years researching the effect of cool air on body preservation. In the cave, he stored a coffin filled with alcohol and then sealed in a copper tube. The coffin was said to hold the body of McDowell's daughter, who died young, although the identity of the dead woman has never been confirmed. Ruffians later broke into the cave and opened the coffin to gawp and gape at the body, and McDowell finally removed it to a safer place. The story was well known around Hannibal and caught the attention of young Sam Clemens/Mark Twain, who would later mention the story in his writings and include a grave-robbing scene in *The Adventures of Tom Sawyer*. Clemens was familiar with McDowell's history through a relative who attended McDowell's medical school and may have helped with the grave robbing. (The Mark Twain Cave, as it is known, is still open for tours.)

During the Civil War, McDowell remained a staunch supporter of the Southern cause and left St. Louis for the Confederate states, where he served variously as a surgeon and spokesperson. His college was seized by Union troops and turned into the hellhole known as Gratiot Prison (after the local street name), where diseases were rampant and death was common among Confederate troops and sympathizers. After the war, McDowell received a presidential pardon and reopened the medical school, where he worked until his death in 1868. Despite his lifelong railing at the Pope's College and the church, McDowell converted to Catholicism before he died. Perhaps nothing reveals better the personality of the man—and his dark humor—than a graduation lecture in which he spoke of his own death:

> *Gentlemen, we have now been together for five long months and we have passed many pleasant and delightful moments together, and doubtless some sad*

and perplexing ones, and now the saddest of all sad words are to be uttered, namely, "Farewell"…In after years one of your number will come back to the City of St. Louis, with the snow of many winters upon his hair, walking not on two legs, but on three, as Sphinx has it, and as he wanders here and there upon the thoroughfares of this great city, suddenly, gentlemen, it will occur to him to ask about Dr. McDowell. Then he will hail and ask one of the eager passersby: "Where is Dr. McDowell," he will say: "What Dr. McDowell?" "Why, Dr. McDowell, the surgeon." He will tell him, gentlemen, that Dr. McDowell lies buried out at Bellefontaine. Slowly and painfully he will wend his way thither. There he will find amidst rank weeds and seeding grass a simple marble slab inscribed, "J.N. McDowell, Surgeon." As he stands there contemplating the rare virtues and eccentricities of this old man, suddenly, gentlemen, the spirit of Dr. McDowell will arise upon ethereal wings and bless him. Yes, thrice bless him. Then it will take a swoop, and when it passes this building, it will drop a parting tear, but, gentlemen, when it gets to Pope's College, it will expectorate.

Chapter 7

Missouri Harmony

Lo, what an entertaining sight,
Are Brethren that agree;
Brethren whose cheerful hearts unite
In bands of harmony.
—from "Union"

Among the music styles associated with Missouri are the Kansas City blues, ragtime, early jazz and fiddle tunes, but Missouri also contributed to the oldest continuing musical tradition in the United States. Shape note singing, *fa-so-la*, patent notes, buckwheat notes: the style goes by many names and is today referred to as sacred harp singing, after the title of a famous tune book. But long before the *Sacred Harp* was published there was *The Missouri Harmony*, whose musical story began in New England, followed the migrant trails west and continues today.

It was 1809 when the *Missouri Gazette* announced something entirely new for the territory: the publication of hymns and psalms in *The Lexington Collection*. The man behind this work was St. Louisan Joseph Charless, who may have published the book at an earlier date while living in Kentucky and then reissued the collection once he moved to St. Louis. But however it came to be, *The Lexington Collection* represented the first Missouri book for Christian singers, as well as a continuation of a revolution in American song. Church music in America had a long history, arriving with the earliest immigrants, but the English tradition decayed rapidly once it stepped onto American shores. Few people were trained in music or could read notes, so during church services, the parson or minister would call out the name of the hymn and then "line out" the tune, singing or even chanting the words to be repeated by the congregation. The resulting drone was generally so awful that educated people who appreciated music found the singing a challenge to their spirits. "Mutilated, tortured and twisted" is how one divine described the badly sung and limited number of tunes he suffered through each Sabbath.

By 1640, a group of ministers had rebelled against the lack of tunes and compiled and published the first book printed in America: *The Bay Psalm Book*. But even that worthy collection of tunes (some of which are still sung today) caused controversy: should church tunes be lively? Should women sing? Were tunes composed by man as worthy as those inspired by God? These theological and musical issues were debated and eventually settled, and *The Bay Psalm Book* was accepted for congregational or group singing. Composers such as the one-eyed tanner William Billings from Massachusetts and the Edson family of Woodstock, New York, composed psalms, hymns, anthems and secular tunes, and by the early nineteenth century, psalm singing was as much a social event as it was part of worship. But in rural areas and on the frontier, learning to sing was more challenging, and singing schools were created in order to fill the gap in musical training.

Singing schools traveled west with migrants and were held in St. Louis as early as 1820. In May 1820, Allen D. Carden, a Tennessean, appeared in St. Louis and advertised a school to be held May 30, when "gentlemen and ladies of this town, who wish to acquire a knowledge of this art, are hereby respectfully informed that an opportunity is now presented them." Classes were held at the Baptist church every Tuesday and Friday at three o'clock and then later by candlelight. In singing schools, the teachers were often self-taught or had taken a school themselves and received a diploma notifying all that the scholar was capable and qualified to hold classes. Some of the men (who dominated the field) had excellent voices and were trained musicians; others learned their work through trial and error. But communities were often deeply appreciative that a teacher would travel the distance to stay and teach.

The school was usually held after the harvest or in winter or early spring before planting began. The class gathered for several weeks in the later afternoon or evening, with students carrying in their own candles, food and foot warmers wherever the classes were held. (Some churches did not want schools held on their premises, so the schoolteacher did the next best thing and booked a classroom at the tavern.) A scholar held a barrel cover on his or her lap to support the songbook and hold the candle in place for reading. Each week, the teacher reviewed topics, including reading music, training the voice and interpreting the text, and then the class began to learn songs in three- or four-part harmony. The songs were often named for a biblical site (Canaan or Jerusalem), a place of importance to the composer (Greenland) or psalms that provided the text. The lyrics reflected the difficulty of life at the time, assuring singers and listeners that despite this world's sorrows, there would be glory in the next. Sometimes, gloomy lyrics were paired with lively tunes, making for an unusual listening experience:

> *Hark from the tombs a doleful sound,*
> *Mine ears attend the cry;*
> *Ye living men come view the ground*
> *Where you must shortly lie.*

Carden, like other teachers, employed a style of musical notation that appealed to people who could not read music. The odd-looking music used "shape notes" or "patent notes" (some of the shapes were registered with the U.S. Patent Office by the composers) to indicate pitch. The scale ran *fa, so, la, fa, so, la, mi, fa,* and there were four shapes to indicate the syllables: a triangle or flag, a "cup," a round note and a diamond. For those who could not read music, the shapes alerted the singer to the intervals between the notes, and therefore, it was not necessary to know whether you were looking at an A# or C. Shape notes had the additional benefit of flexibility;

singers did not have to worry about keys because the intervals or sounds would remain the same no matter if one sang high or low. In addition, songs were listed in hymnbooks along with their meter or time signature. So any songs in common meter, for example, could be sung to any tune with a common meter, leading to many variations. The singing teacher taught the class how to read the intervals, how to count the notes and how to determine the tempo or speed of the piece. He would then set the pitch so it was comfortable for the singers, start the song and beat time with a flat-handed, up-and-down movement.

Although teachers traveled to Missouri from the South and the East, much fun was made of the latter, especially when they sang with a nasal New England twang. One frontier Missourian joked about how a friend saved him from a grizzly attack by singing:

> *When Jonas and myself were returning to our main camp from a long hunt, with our horses well laden with beaver and traps, we met a white barr* [grizzly] *in an open prairie… He came on, with mouth open, to within fifteen steps of us, then halted and stood up to look…Jonas was not quite so steady in his* narves *as I could have wished, for he was unused to the varmints, and his gun cracked a little too soon. My nag threw up her head, and my gun went off before I got a fine sight. "Now," said I, "Jonas we are in*

a pretty fix. Try your best in psalm-singing—it's our only chance!" Jonas bellowed out all sorts of base, *and I wasn't far behind him. I had taken a hand at hymns, lined off in camp-meetings when singers and* converts war skase. *The barr* tuck *a right good look at us, and then broke for high timber.*

In addition to the Missouri singing school (possibly the first west of the Mississippi River), Allen Carden's contribution to music was the publication of a new tune book, *The Missouri Harmony or a Choice Collection of Psalm Tunes, Hymns, and Anthems, Selected from the Most Eminent Authors, and Well Adapted to all Christian Churches, Singing Schools and Private Societies.* Carden was well respected by singing school teachers, and he both acknowledged and borrowed text and tunes from books by friends and colleagues. *The Missouri Harmony* contained hymns and psalms that drew from folk tunes, jigs, Celtic songs and lively, multi-voiced "anthems," which offered sophisticated harmonies, jangling rhythms and musical plays on words and tune. The songs included classics such as "Old Hundred," "All Hail the Power of Jesus' Name" and "Captain Kidd." In the latter, new words praised God even as the original song mourned the career and death of a pirate. Shape note tunes were often fast, loud and colorful, covering such topics as the river Jordan (which echoed with Missourians in their river-bound state), death and changing seasons:

We have a howling wilderness,
To Canaan's happy shore,
A land of dearth and pits and snares
Where chilling winds doth roar.
—from "Pilgrim"

Although Carden titled his collection *The Missouri Harmony*, he faced a daunting problem printing the book: a shape note font was not available in St. Louis. So Carden had *The Missouri Harmony* printed in Cincinnati, at the time a center for book and printing arts. *The Missouri Harmony* quickly became one of the foundation texts for sacred music in America. Copies of the book were sold throughout the South, the Midwest, Indiana and Illinois, where, according to legend, Abraham Lincoln and his sweetheart, Ann Rutledge, sang from the book at Illinois gatherings and Lincoln parodied the song "How Tedious and Tasteless the Hours" with off-color versions.

Today, shape note groups continue to meet and share music in Missouri, and an annual convention of singers attracts hundreds to the songs and the traditional picnic lunch "dinner on the grounds." *The Missouri Harmony* is still used around the world and has been reissued in an updated version, ensuring that the rousing and joyful singing will continue to keep alive the sound of Missouri's past.

Chapter 8

Two Janes

One born in Missouri and left to make her fortune and infamy; the other was born in Kentucky but associated with Hannibal, Missouri. The first was a colorful, bawdy, profane adventuress; the latter was a funny, lively storyteller. One was a calamity and the other a mother of American literature.

Calamity Jane

Martha Jane Canary was famous for many things: Deadwood, North Dakota, sharpshooting, drinking. Her life was difficult and harsh, and from childhood on, she made her own way. Journalists, whiskey and others who sought to benefit from her fame fabricated much of her personal history. A true legend, Jane was a blend of fact, fiction and self-invention.

Martha's parents were Robert W. and Charlotte Canary, who settled in Princeton, Mercer County, Missouri. Charlotte was sixteen years old at Martha's birth on May 1, 1852, and had at least three children by the time she was twenty. The Canary family, including Robert's father and other relatives, migrated to Missouri from Ohio and Iowa and purchased farming land. Martha may have been born in her grandfather's log cabin, but her exact birthplace is unknown. The family chose a region more abolitionist than other parts of the state and a rather isolated area at that; at least one history claimed that no white famers had moved to Mercer County before 1837, a mere fifteen years before the Canarys arrived. Most settlers in the region planted corn and other crops and were self-sufficient.

Almost nothing is known about Martha's childhood, but some of the stories recalled by her neighbors in later years might give a hint at her heritage. Robert Canary appeared to be successful as long as his father, James, was alive to guide him, but once James passed away, Robert again moved the family west, perhaps to the gold fields. Charlotte was considered less than a lady given that she smoked, used strong language and enjoyed drinking; at least one story told by a relative said that Robert met Charlotte when she was working as a soiled dove in a bawdyhouse. A rather simple soul, he fell in love and married her, to the shock of family and neighbors.

By 1864, Robert and Charlotte were in debt and decided to move the family to Montana Territory. The family fared very badly there, and a newspaper report from the time mentions several children who were found destitute and begging for assistance. The children included Martha, and her parents were castigated in print for their poverty. Martha helped her mother take in washing and was recalled as a pretty, lively girl. (Other stories say she was much too popular with the men for her own good.) Not long after, Charlotte died from pneumonia. Robert and the children then set out for Utah Territory with a dream of homesteading, but once again, tragedy changed Martha's life: Robert died, leaving the six children to fend for themselves. Martha cared for the family the best she could, but in 1868 at sixteen, she moved to Wyoming Territory.

The few existing photographs of a young Martha show a dark-haired woman of middle height, with strong features and a direct gaze. Some called her pretty, while others thought she was homely. (One of her friends was the shady lady Madame Mustache, so Jane may have been considered quite handsome next to the company she kept.) Although Martha was photographed several times in trousers, buckskin and a felt hat, she also dressed in lace, ruffles, feathers and elaborate, curled hairdos. She worked at many jobs: scout, railroad worker and, most likely, prostitute. She traveled in wagon trains, wrangled horses and did all the work men did. According to one story, when she was twenty, Martha was involved in a skirmish with Indians and was credited with saving a military officer after he was shot. He is said to have given her the nickname "Calamity Jane," since he was so lucky in having her around during a calamity. Another story said that she was such a character, anyone who married her would marry a calamity, and the nickname stuck. Or perhaps she said "Calamity!" when she lost at cards. The stories are many, but Calamity Jane became her name.

Jane was as well known for her drinking and carousing as anyone on the frontier. At one point, her sister refused to allow Jane to visit her nieces and nephews, fearing Jane's language and influence on the children. But she was more than a colorful joke. During one epidemic, Jane nursed the miners through illness, giving little thought to her own safety. And she certainly earned respect and some affection. Jane had a number of relationships, including at least one marriage. She was a good shot, a good horsewoman and an alcoholic. Her fame came from journalists, who spun her stories into dime novels and newspaper articles filled with amazing lies. Jane was probably best known for her friendship with Wild Bill Hickok. The two met on a wagon train, and while it is not known whether there was an affair, Jane later claimed that Wild Bill was the father of her child, whom she later gave up for adoption. (Wild Bill is another Missouri legend. In 1865, Bill and Davis Tutt got into an altercation over poker debts. The resulting shootout was the first quick-draw gun battle in public. Hickok killed Tutt and was acquitted.)

In her later years, Jane eked out a living selling photographs of herself while appearing in wild West shows and at events such as the Pan-American Exposition. She died in 1903, possibly from alcohol poisoning, and was buried next to Wild Bill Hickok. No one knows whether the burial was arranged because of a need for tourism, a posthumous joke on Hickok (who was once said to have detested Jane) or because she truly cared for the man. There was never anything simple or clear about Jane's life and history, but she was an independent woman who lived through difficult times, and her story still holds an important place in the cultural history of the American West.

JANE LAMPTON CLEMENS

Born in 1803 in Kentucky, Jane Lampton was descended from pioneers eccentric and quirky. Her great-aunt survived an Indian attack and gained fame as a swift-footed heroine; her grandfather was buried in his favorite chair, secured in a coffin built with cherry wood meant for her grandmother's parlor. Jane's parents were beautiful, feckless and unskilled in day-to-day living, loving their daughters but allowing them to run wild in a time when a lady was expected to ride sidesaddle and work needlepoint. When Jane's mother passed away, her stepmother attempted to change the high-spirited girl into a quiet young woman and failed miserably. Jane and her sister Patsy were the local belles, and Jane was known as the finest horsewoman in the state, an excellent dancer and a superb mimic. While she had many suitors, Jane gave her heart to a young man studying to become a doctor and expected his proposal any day. One story told that the young man mentioned his intentions to Jane's uncle, and Jane was offended by the breach of confidentiality and refused to see her beau again. But whatever happened, Jane and the young man went their separate ways, and in 1823, she married a quiet, reserved young lawyer named John Clemens. Try as John did, he could not make a go of the legal world in Kentucky or later in Tennessee, so he decided to migrate to Missouri along with his wife and young children.

The Clemens family first lived on a farm near present-day Florida, Missouri, where Jane gave birth on November 30, 1835, to a frail and premature infant she despaired of surviving the harsh winter. Samuel Langhorne was named for John's father and a family friend, and he was sickly and near enough to death many times that few thought he would make it beyond boyhood, much less to manhood. "A lady came in one day," Jane Clemens once recalled to her family, and "said you don't expect to raise that babe do you? I said I would try. But he was a poor looking object to raise."

Jane and John's marriage was an unhappy one, a union of two opposites. John was severe, anxious, a man who simply couldn't make business work for him, but a man who had vision and community service in his blood.

Jane was fun-loving, caring, a storyteller who enjoyed a good joke and tried to stay one step ahead of Sam. Sam recalled that his parents were "courteous, considerate and always respectful," kind to each other but never warm or affectionate. Once again, John's business failed, and he moved the family to Hannibal in order to be closer to legal work. The family lived in a house made famous by *The Adventures of Tom Sawyer*, and Sam recalled trying to avoid his mother's attempts to "civilize" him.

Sam and Jane shared much of the same personality: wit, a love of music and the ability to see humor. In a 1928 news article, a childhood friend of Sam Clemens recalled Jane:

> *Mrs. Clemens was never fond of housekeeping. The monotony of it bored her. She often said she did not believe in doing anything that was disagreeable if you could help it. The things she liked to do she pursued with diligence, such as quilt making and embroidery. These domestic arts she practiced to almost the end of her days and she lived to be past 87. In all her likes and dislikes Mrs. Clemens was quite decided. She cared for almost anything spectacular—parades, picnics, circuses, and shows of all kinds. She found delight in going to market, enjoyed mingling with people and bringing them home with her. Her house was filled with guests oftener perhaps than she could afford.*

Throughout his life, Sam teased Jane unmercifully, perhaps realizing how much he resembled her in personality. One day at the Hannibal house, Sam bet his brother that Jane was so softhearted she would defend even Satan. Sam proceeded to insult and revile Satan in Jane's hearing until she could take it no longer and said that of the sinners who needed prayers, Satan was the most deserving. Sam collected his bet. Sam's reputation for stretching the truth was well known around Hannibal, and although Jane could not cure his tale-telling, she learned to manage it, according to Sam:

> *When I was seven or eight, or ten, or twelve years old—along there—a neighbor said to her* [my mother], *"Do you ever believe anything that that boy says?" My mother said, "He is the well-spring of truth, but you can't bring up the whole well with one bucket"—and she added, "I know his average, therefore he never deceives me. I discount him thirty per cent for embroidery, and what is left is perfect and priceless truth, without a flaw in it anywhere."*

John Clemens failed again to build a successful business, and the family slid into poverty. Then, on his way home in 1847 after a trip to sell some land, John caught a chill and died. Jane never remarried and struggled to keep her family together. She lived the remainder of her life with her son Orion and daughter Pamela in Missouri,

WHO IS THE REAL
MARK TWAIN?
JANE CLEMENS

Iowa and New York. Despite the loss of four children and widowhood, Jane remained undefeated by grief or poverty and was thrilled by Sam's writings as Mark Twain. He recalled that Jane loved life and was young at heart, and he told stories about her indomitable will to raise him to manhood as honest and upright as Tom Sawyer would be someday. Here, Twain recalled the sugar bowl incident with his brother Henry and Jane:

> *One day when she was not present, Henry took sugar from her prized and precious old English sugar-bowl, which was an heirloom in the family—and he managed to break the bowl. It was the first time I had ever had a chance to tell anything on him, and I was inexpressibly glad. I told him I was going to tell on him, but he was not disturbed. When my mother came in and saw the bowl lying on the floor in fragments, she was speechless for a minute. I allowed that silence to work; I judged it would increase the effect. I was waiting for her to ask "Who did that?"—so that I could fetch out my news. But it was an error of calculation. When she got through with her silence she didn't ask anything about it—she merely gave me a crack on the skull with her thimble that I felt all the way down to my heels. Then I broke out with my injured innocence, expecting to make her very sorry that she had punished the wrong one. She said, without emotion, "It's all right. It isn't any matter.*

You deserve it for something you've done that I didn't know about; and if you haven't done it, why then you deserve it for something that you are going to do, that I sha'n't hear about."

That Jane survived her son's plots and plans spoke well of her patience and understanding of what it meant to be a boy:

Those were the cholera days of '49. The people along the Mississippi were paralyzed with fright. Those who could run away, did it…Those who couldn't flee kept themselves drenched with cholera preventives, and my mother chose Perry Davis's Pain-Killer for me. She was not distressed about herself. But she made me promise to take a teaspoonful of Pain-Killer every day…She marked my bottle with a pencil, on the label, every day, and examined it to see if the teaspoonful had been removed. The floor was not carpeted. It had cracks in it, and I fed the Pain-Killer to the cracks with very good results—no cholera occurred down below.

Jane saw Sam infrequently after he gained fame, but mother and son corresponded until her death in 1890. Her earlier, frugal life had taught Jane to waste nothing, and she would often write notes to Sam on scraps of paper. After years of this, Sam tired of trying to read the cramped writing and finally tried to cure her of the habit. He wrote Jane a letter on fresh paper as well as on old correspondence, tore it all up, stuffed it into an envelope and sent it off to her to puzzle out.

Jane Clemens is buried in the Mount Olivet Cemetery in Hannibal, Missouri. She lives on as Aunt Polly in *Tom Sawyer* and in the memory of American readers. She certainly stayed in the heart of her son:

> *I was always told that I was a sickly and precarious and tiresome and uncertain child, and lived mainly on allopathic medicines during the first seven years of my life. I asked my mother about this, in her old age and said:*
>
> *I suppose that during all that time you were uneasy about me?*
>
> *Yes, the whole time.*
>
> *Afraid I wouldn't live?*
>
> *After a reflective pause—ostensibly to think out the facts—*
>
> *No—afraid you would.*

Chapter 9

HOME SWEET UTOPIA

The search for the perfect life has a long and odd history, but nowhere more so than in the state of Missouri. Back in territory days, the Boonslick country in central Missouri was the goal of settlers in search of milk, honey and good land. Of course, the reality was more in the way of mosquitoes, floods and good land, but the Boonslick still drew hundreds of settlers hoping for a new start in a new state. In 1838, Joseph Smith announced to the Latter-Day Saints that the Garden of Eden was located in the northwest corner of Missouri. He named the site Adam-ondi-Ahman, and members of the LDS Church believed that was where they would gather for the second coming of their savior. The nineteenth century was also a time when the idea of creating the perfect community arose, places where all people were social, economic and cultural equals. The settlements and groups where people hoped to create a perfect world were called utopian communities (from the Greek, meaning both "nowhere" and "good place"), and these communes were found in the transcendentalism of New England; the river settlement of New Harmony, Indiana; the wilds of Kansas; and, of course, in Missouri. But as with much of Missouri's history, nothing was as it seemed—especially perfection.

HARMONY

Wilhelm Keil was born in Prussia in 1812, the son of a linen weaver. He trained as a tailor and an herbalist as a young man, learning the secrets of natural healing. Always drawn to religion and mysticism, Keil decided to bring his family to New York in 1836 after being told to leave his homeland by a Roma seeress. The Keils eventually moved on to Pittsburgh, where he set up shop and was known as "doctor" by his patients. During these years, Keil apparently underwent several religious conversions and considered becoming a Methodist minister, but his belief that a minister should not be paid put him at odds with the church. Keil turned his interests to communal groups, especially the Harmony Society, founded by George Rapp in southern Indiana. Keil was described as a powerful speaker who convinced audiences to leave their current lives and join him in a Christian, communal life. By 1844, Keil was searching for a place to found a colony and settled on the area that is now Bethel in Shelby County, north central Missouri.

The commune members came from across the Midwest and were willing to give up their homes, their personal goods and the traditional family structure in order to receive what Keil promised: hard work, bread, water and fellowship. His followers were devoted to Keil, and his was the final word in legal, spiritual and community matters. Supporters called him Doctor or Father Keil, while detractors dubbed him King Keil. Reports of Keil's life—especially by Charles Nordhoff in 1875—claim that Keil used magnetism for healing and that he owned a book written in human blood. The latter held many medical receipts for curing, and Keil later burned the book in public. (It is possible this book was a grimoire, a book of magic spells.) Whatever the outside world thought of him, Keil was a charismatic leader whose word was law. The Bethel German Colony, as it was called, faced many difficulties during the harsh Missouri winters and springs, but soon a town grew, with large community halls, brick homes and churches.

The colony thrived under Keil's direction, growing to nearly seven hundred members mostly of German heritage, who worked to provide food, clothing and housing for one another. The colony maintained a number of successful businesses, including milling, a distillery and textile production. The houses were simply furnished, and as one visitor noted, "Everything is clean, the beds are neat," although he criticized the lack of labor-saving devices.

Families were expected to raise their own produce, as well as enough to share or sell, and a portion of the income was set aside for care of the infirm and aged.

Keil's home was a large, three-story brick structure named Elim, located outside the main village. (Elim was where the Israelites rested after crossing the Red Sea.) From this grand house, Keil ran the colony, compounded his herbs for the community pharmacy and met with and entertained townspeople. The colonists were hardworking, frugal and serious, but they enjoyed holidays and events, including Christmas, Easter, the harvest and Keil's birthday on March 6. That day was particularly special, a time when everyone joined in processions, listened to the colony band and participated in singing, dancing and dining in the second-floor banquet room of Elim.

Keil ruled as a visionary mystic, and the community followed and flourished. Bethel did not allow slavery during a time when that marked them as abolitionists in a slave state. Much like the Shakers, the colonists' world was one of simplicity and sharing, but Keil was ever vigilant regarding the intrusion of the modern world on Bethel. By 1855, Keil had decided to move west and begin an offshoot colony that would be far from the civil unrest and the effect it had on the Latter-Day Saints, the abolitionists and other Missouri groups. He selected Oregon as his next destination and sent out a scouting trip. Once a site was located, fifty-five founding colonists agreed to follow. Keil's eldest son, Willie, had wanted to join the scouts but couldn't because of illness, so Keil promised him that when the main exodus began, Willie would ride in the lead wagon. In a devastating blow to Keil, Willie died only days before the main group left. A grieving Keil placed Willie in a wooden, lead-lined coffin and filled it with Golden Rule whiskey, which was distilled at the colony. The coffin was placed in a wagon, and the group started off. Father Keil said that he "knew" Willie would protect the wagon train from danger and from Indian tribes who fought to stem white migration. Curious Native Americans stopped the wagon train several times and asked to see the boy. One time, Keil opened the coffin and the Germans sang a dirge for Willie; the Indians listened quietly and then left the migrants in peace. A few Indians remained with the wagon train and acted as guides through some of the roughest territory. The colonists arrived safely in Oregon, Keil having kept his promise to his son, who was buried in Oregon.

Keil directed both the Aurora Colony in Oregon and the Bethel Colony until his death in 1877. Over the years, hundreds of people left Bethel for Oregon, especially when civil war was imminent. By the 1870s, Bethel had only two hundred inhabitants, while several other families lived nearby in a colony called Nineveh. Bethel had passed its glory days, although the remaining families continued to work as coopers, tinsmiths, weavers and farmers. The wool factory and the distillery had burned down, and no move was made to rebuild them. The land was divided among members of the community, but no one filed their deeds for years, and it was still maintained under communal ownership. Once Father Keil's guidance was gone, the community faced indecision and disagreement. The Bethel Colony disbanded in 1879, although the community lived on as a thriving Missouri village, which today contains historic sites recalling a time when harmony grew from the land.

LIBERAL MISSOURI

While Father Keil and Bethel followed the Bible as a guide for living, another communal group in Missouri took a very different direction: Liberal, Missouri, was founded as a haven for atheists. The *Sikeston Herald* reported in the early twentieth century:

> The founder of this unique community experiment, George H. Walser, was born in Indiana in 1834. He went to Barton county immediately after the war, where he was soon recognized as one of the best lawyers in southwest Missouri. He was elected prosecuting attorney there, and became a member of the 25th assembly. With an eye for future developments he purchased 2,000 acres of land and selected the site of Liberal as the home of an experiment in intellectual community living. He was an agnostic and placed himself in open opposition to organized religion. "With one foot upon the neck of priestcraft and the other upon the rock of truth," he declared, "we have thrown our banner to the breeze and challenge the world to produce a better cause for the devotion of man than that of a grand, noble and perfect humanity."

Advertisements for Liberal offered a place where there would be "no priest, preachers, saloon, God, or Hell." True to its name, the community held open forums for discussion of philosophy, religion and culture that would lead, it was hoped, to "free, intelligent thought." As described in a town history, "In the Mental Liberty Hall lectures were given each Sunday evening, and scientists, philosophers, socialists, atheists, Protestant ministers and Catholic priests were invited to speak—respectable decorum being the only limitation placed upon any speaker." Science classes were offered to children and youth on a weekly basis with a goal of freeing people from the bias of a single theology. Of course, Liberal attracted much attention. Missionaries purchased nearby land and founded the town of Pedro in defiance of George Walser, who erected barbed-wire fences around Liberal in order to keep out Christians. The missionaries fired back with signs that read "And the Lord said, Get thee out of Sodom." Newspapers carried articles condemning the "Liberals" as hypocrites with few morals who lived in sin. The community accepted those who lived together without benefit of marriage, free thinkers, books on radical subjects and, apparently, birth control (the families of the "infidels" averaged only one child each, a low birth rate for the time).

Later in life, Walser embraced spiritualism and built a beautiful thirteen-acre camp called Catalpa Park with cottages, tents and housing for meetings. Mediums and others interested in breaking the veil between this world and the next flocked to Liberal every summer. One of the most famous scandals to shake the spiritualist world

took place in Liberal. Dr. J.B. Bouton led séances that gained large followings, but after a fire in a building, Bouton was unmasked as a fraud: his "spirits" entered the room through a trapdoor. Walser did not hide the scandal, instead revealing it to all in the town. Bouton became a pariah and later wrote a book, *Two Years Among the Spirits in the Godless Town of Liberal: The Experience of the Famous Medium*, in which he defended his fraud by claiming to have done so in order to "cure" the town of its belief in spiritualism:

> *The question arose in my mind how to produce a spook. A thought struck me. I sat with my side to the circle, threw my arm out, raised my hand above my head and brought it forward to the door, when one of the party exclaimed: "O, there she is!" All...believed it to be the spirit of the deceased landlady. Finally I took a white handkerchief in my hand and brought it forward. They could then see every feature plainly—one party saw the same dress she wore before she died and even the pleats in the dress.*

Ever the open-minded thinker, by the end of his life, Walser had changed philosophical direction once again, embracing Christianity and writing for the public about his conversion. He died in 1910 at Catalpa Park, and his Liberal experiment ended, but the story of the town that allowed neither heaven nor hell to rule is still told.

Chapter 10

MURDER WILL OUT

Murder in Missouri was no different from murder anywhere else, if the newspapers in the nineteenth century were to be believed: driven by greed, lust, revenge and madness, killers hacked, shot or strangled people to death. Sometimes the local horror turned to rage and the murderer was lynched by hanging, considered a swift and well-deserved justice by the community. National and local newspapers reported the murders in lurid detail, portraying Missouri as an outlaw borderland where guns and knives were common and revenge—in the form of the law— was as brutal as the crime. But now and again, a murder occurred that was macabre beyond understanding. The Le Blanc legend horrified St. Louis in the 1870s and still resonates more than 140 years later.

It was a hot, enervating July afternoon in Jefferson County, Missouri, not far from modern-day Crystal City, and a dark-eyed, merry young woman was working in her flower garden. Julie Le Blanc descended from an old and regal French line; her father was a well-to-do farmer who settled among the French communities along the Mississippi River where Crystal (now Plattin) Creek meandered through farmland and woods. Dressed in a lovely gown and the family jewelry, Julie was picking flowers for a bouquet and waiting for her escort, James Leonard, to take her to a neighbor's party. The young couple were said to be happy together, and Julie's family expected an engagement announcement by the end of the year.

The Le Blanc family gave it little thought when Julie did not return in the evening, believing she had remained with her friends, a common event in the days when dances could last through the night. But when Julie did not return the next day, the family contacted their neighbors and Julie's associates. No one had seen her, and she had not attended the dance at all. In fact, James had planned all along to escort his sister to the party as well, but when he did not see Julie waiting at the gate, he assumed she had remained home because of illness.

Julie's disappearance shocked the town, and search parties scoured the nearby woods and riverbanks. The local men were excellent trackers and hunters, and they soon picked up a trail: footprints of a woman's shoe, which matched Julie's, and the footprint of an unknown man. The tracks led to the creek, where Julie's father had kept a cooper-bottomed craft known as a lifeboat. Once there, the searchers discovered that the line had been loosened and no boat was to be seen. Julie and her companion had disappeared into thin air, and the family was distraught. Perhaps she had run off with a lover? There was no indication of force, but all thought James Leonard was her sweetheart, and he had been far away from the house. Julie was known as a happy, loving girl, and she might have given her heart to another young man on impulse. A search was made up and down the stream and the Mississippi banks, but no trace was found of the couple. The family hoped Julie would return soon a married woman and with many apologies for the distress she had caused, but after months of waiting, Julie's grief-stricken parents finally accepted that their daughter had gone from them.

Another victim of Julie's loss was her childhood friend Philip Kenealy, who helped in the search. He came to the family sometime after her disappearance and told the Le Blancs that living in the neighborhood where Julie and he had played as children was taking a terrible toll on his spirit. He announced that he was leaving the village and moving to New Orleans to accept a position in a wholesale store. Julie's mother was heartbroken to see him go—after all, he had been a part of their family from childhood—but he could not be persuaded to remain and took a steamboat downriver. Soon after Kenealy's departure—perhaps due to parental intuition—Mr. Le Blanc came to believe that Kenealy might have known something about Julie's whereabouts. He sent detectives to New Orleans to question Kenealy, but to no avail: the young man had disappeared.

Six years later, in the spring of 1878, Benjamin F. Aiken, a farmhand, was hunting snipe near Point Pleasant along the Mississippi banks at New Madrid. He noticed a small skiff drifting free with the current, and using a pole, Aiken was able to draw in the boat as it moved toward the shore. The craft was nearly filled with rainwater, and another storm would have sent it to the bottom forever. Aiken was horrified at what he found in the boat, which was described in the *St. Louis Evening Post*: "a ghastly, grinning skeleton…The bones had been bleached by the sun and rain until they were of a pure snowy whiteness, and as the sun shone down on them so polished were they that it was painful to look at them." An old tarp lay rotting in the rainwater, and tie ropes dangled from the boat. Aiken found a gold pin and gold bracelets in the bottom of the boat. Rain and river seepage had washed the jewelry, but it was clear that the bracelets had animals and other designs carved into them. Aiken secured the boat to shore, collected the jewelry and went to find help. The police and the local coroner, Isaac Tebbets, considered there was little to be done except to bury the bones along the riverbank and take the jewelry for safekeeping.

Not long after, word of the discovery reached Mr. Le Blanc upriver. He traveled to Point Pleasant, where he viewed the jewelry. The gold pieces he identified as his family's heirlooms, so the body must have been that of Julie who had disappeared so long ago. The horrified father made arrangements to exhume Julie's remains and bring her back home for a proper burial, but on searching for the grave, he discovered that the riverbank had collapsed into the water and stolen Julie from the family forever.

And the killer? Until his dying day, Le Blanc accused Philip Kenealy of the murder. It all made sense: Julie would only leave with someone she knew. Kenealy must have lured her into the boat and then strangled her in a jealous rage, hiding the boat under dense brush until he could escape. A stranger would have taken the gold and sold it, but Kenealy knew that it would be instantly recognized by the villagers. Of course, he was never heard from again despite much national publicity about the case. But as the local papers pointed out, "Time makes all things clear," and the legend of the skeleton in the skiff was told for many years along the Mississippi.

Chapter 11

Scoundrel

The Lost Life of Alphonso Wetmore

Never was a frontier Missouri character so outrageous—and so forgotten. Alphonso Wetmore—military man, writer, journalist, humorist, politician, Santa Fe trader, playwright and lawyer—blew into the Missouri territory in 1819 and, at his death thirty years later, left behind a rich bequest of humor, short stories and history. Among the first of the western humorists, Wetmore was a literary uncle of later writers like Mark Twain, but few now recall Wetmore's role in Missouri history.

Alphonso Wetmore was born on February 17, 1793, in Winchester, Connecticut. His parents, Seth and Lois, had deep roots in New England, ten children and countless relations. Seth served in the War for Independence and later publicly defended the extension of suffrage to all men, stating that "every man who is 21 years of age and pays taxes has a natural right to vote." He was branded a radical by wealthy landowners and prosecuted under the alien and sedition laws, so in 1803, Seth moved his family to New York's Mohawk Valley frontier. Little is known of Alphonso's early life, although his fictionalized "autobiography" written in the 1830s provides some hints. Alphonso Wetmore was schooled in history and literature, studied law and was a fan of Washington Irving's books and stories. When the War of 1812 began, Wetmore joined the army and served along the Niagara frontier during the early brutal battles. In competition with another New York soldier and friend, Robert Morris, Wetmore courted Mary Smith from Ames, New York. Before the two young men left for battle, they competed for a miniature portrait of the young lady, all in good fun; Wetmore was the victor and claimed the prize. Only weeks later, Morris was killed on October 13, 1812, in a vicious ambush by the British. Wetmore survived, barely, suffering shrapnel wounds and losing his arm to a cannonball. He always maintained that he survived the blast because the shrapnel struck the portrait, which he kept in a pocket over his heart. In a fitting end to the sadness, Alphonso and Mary were married soon after he recovered.

Wetmore was eventually promoted and, after the war ended, continued his military career in the Sixth Infantry despite his injuries. He wrote with his left hand, hunted, rode horses and mules and was a good shot with rifles and pistols. The Sixth was posted to the frontier, and in 1819, Wetmore and family moved by keelboat, raft and wagon to the Missouri town of Franklin, where he settled his wife and children. He quickly became involved in Franklin's social and cultural life, contributing funds to a library, school and gristmill, but his most lasting influence on Missouri history was essays written for the local newspaper, the *Missouri Intelligencer and Boonslick Advertiser.* Here, Wetmore wrote under the pseudonyms "Captain Rainmore," "Random Ranger" and "Aurora Borealis," describing frontier life with verve and humor. One night, he stopped at a local settler's house and was treated to dinner, which Wetmore described with an ear for detail and language:

> *Lieutenant Ranger was supping at the hospitable board of Jehu Roup when the preliminaries of this bear hunt were arranged.*
>
> *"Nelly, my honey," said he, "holp the stranger's plate to another midlin smart smigging of deer meat. Leftenant, do you think Solomon in all his glory ever had better livin than we have, honey and roasted ribs? (will you take another leetle sprinkle of the jirk?) that is to say in the middle of watermillion time, like it is now, with fresh honey and a right good run of new whiskey."*
>
> *"He was certainly very unreasonable to desire any thing better than this substantial fare," said the lieutenant, "and of all the viands I ever tasted, commend me to bear meat and deer ribs, dressed as these are."*
>
> *"They are pretty ostensible," said Jehu Roup.*

Wetmore was one of the earliest Missourians to record stories about the trappers and hunters of the region, including Mike Shuck, who had a trained bear as a pack animal. One day, Wetmore invited Shuck into his house, and to Wetmore's delight, the bear came along as well and made itself comfortable on the bed.

Wetmore's travels took him from St. Louis and Franklin to Nebraska, Kansas, Santa Fe, Washington, New York, Pennsylvania and Florida and from the Red River to the Missouri, riding, boating and walking thousands of miles a year. He was invited to the White House to dine with President and Mrs. Madison and other 1812 war veterans. At one point, he nearly drowned when his raft sank during a storm on the Missouri River, but despite his heavy uniform and the use of only one arm, he managed to get ashore. (On the raft was a strongbox filled with paper money and gold, which sank to the river bottom. Unfortunately for Wetmore, U.S. Congress held him responsible for the loss and demanded repayment.) During the 1820s, Wetmore traveled to Santa Fe as *caravanbachi*, or caravan leader, put down a mutiny among traders and participated in a coup attempt in Chihuahua, Mexico. While he may have exaggerated some of his adventures in writing, still they have a ring of truth to them, including this showdown with a defiant Santa Fe trader:

Mike Terrapin was an indifferent farmer, but a good hunter, and he fancied himself a ready-made merchant. He had accordingly loaded a wagon with goods for the New Mexico trade. In the instance to which we refer, his wagon was at the head of one line when he was ordered by Captain Rainmore in person, to halt.

"Well, maybe I mount, and then again I mou'tent," said he—"I allow to camp over tother side of the branch;" indicating at the same time a determination to put his team again in motion.

"Disengage your team from your wagon instantly," said the captain, "and if you move a yard further ahead, I will give you a buck load." The fearless mutineer took the reins, evidently with the purpose of going ahead. Captain Rainmore raised his double barrel, drew back the cock of each lock, and looked steadily at his victim. There was no evidence of fear in the countenance of Mike Terrapin, but he spread over his visage a muscular movement which he designed should pass for a smile, and remarked—

"I allow, capting, I had better flunk in, for you look reather kantankerous—though there's nary man on this little yearth that I'm afeard of. I'll give in, and ongear."

When Captain Rainmore visited the guards that night at one o'clock, as was his custom, he found Mike Terrapin sitting at his camp fire roasting a marrow bone.

"Is that you, capting," said he, looking up, "I and you will be right good friends arter our little skrimmage to-day, for I like a man to show the raal grit. Let's liquor: here is a little tickler of old corn that will keep the agy off when you're up to your knees in the foggiest kind of a fixin. Capting, here's to the American Eagle and Gineral Jacksing; may they never slope out of a fair fight. You'll find me standing by you in all sorts of ways, any how you can fit it."

Wetmore eventually resigned his commission and moved to St. Louis in 1833. There, he published the first *Gazetteer of Missouri* and was owner and co-publisher of the Missouri *Saturday News* with fur trader Charles Keemle. Wetmore entered politics, practiced law and wrote short stories. He seemed to be a man who made either good friends or devoted enemies. He was often called a scoundrel by his opponents, accused of shady business dealings and hauled into court over debts. Still, he thrived on the rough-and-tumble frontier and refused to be hobbled by his injuries. Ever the adventurer, Wetmore traveled to California in 1849. He returned to St. Louis later that year and died during the cholera epidemic. His grave was moved several times, and today its location is unknown, but he left behind a rare personal record of Missouri's early days.

Chapter 12

The Little Stranger

Yeomen strong, hither throng—
Nature's honest men—
We will make the wildness
Bud and bloom again.
Ho, brothers! Come brothers!
Hasten all with me,
We'll sing, upon the Kansas plains,
The song of liberty.
—by Lucy Larcom, quoted in Went to Kansas

Migrants who headed west in the 1850s did so in hope of a better life, whether they were searching for land, religious freedom or a place free of slavery. Whatever the motivation, migrants often chose their destinations based on news from travelers and journalists, promoters and dreamers who reported a world of rich acreage, balmy weather and bountiful harvests. People followed the sun and hope, leaving behind everything familiar and safe. Some succeeded, many failed, but nearly all suffered the toll of an overland journey through prairie, desert and mountain. Loss of livestock was a tragedy; loss of household goods was heartbreaking. But loss of loved ones was incomprehensible to those who buried parents, spouses and children along the trail with only a rough cross to mark their passing. Miriam Colt had no idea what she faced when she stepped into the West.

In 1856, Miriam Davis Colt, her husband, William H., and their toddlers, Willie and Mema, decided to seek a new life for their family. The Colts were upstate New York farmers and vegetarians, and the hard winters and shorter growing seasons made their way of life difficult and strenuous. Miriam was a forward-thinking woman who embraced the idea of female emancipation and wore the rather scandalous "bloomer dress" consisting of bloomers and a short skirt. A move to a new world might bring even more opportunities for her family, and when the opportunity came, the Colts responded: they joined the Vegetarian Settlement Company and purchased shares for a farm in the new land near the Neosho River (near present-day Canute, Kansas). The company was founded by Henry Stephens Clubb, an Englishman who had been active in the radical movement of vegetarianism. It was Clubb's dream to create a place "where families [could have] their children educated away from the ordinary incentives to vice, vicious company, vicious habits of eating and drinking, and other contaminations of old cities." Clubb boasted of his organization and inspired shareholders, telling them they "must render the Vegetarian Settlement a most desirable place of residence to all whose tastes are averse to those habits of gross indulgence which are degrading to mankind." Those who joined the company signed a pledge:

> *I, _____ do voluntarily agree to abstain from all intoxicating liquors as beverages, from tobacco in every form, and from the flesh of animals; to promote social, moral, and political freedom; to maintain the observance of all good and righteous laws, and to otherwise conform to the rules adopted by a majority of the Vegetarian Settlement Company.*

Clubb gathered more than fifty-five families to his cause, people—including the Colts—who may have been unaware that Clubb lacked the support of either the English or American vegetarian headquarters. Clubb's company was, in effect, a private, communal enterprise directed by a man who had no experience in frontier living and no knowledge of the dangers found along the great migration trails across the country.

The Colts left New York in March and began their long trip west. After the hip-deep snow of late winter, the family must have looked forward to the Eden described in the company's literature:

> *Throughout the Osage country there are scenes of romantic loveliness…Over all, a Sabbath serenity is diffused; and grassy knoll and leafy wood are embathed in a soft and subdued lustre, which is indescribably soothing, and inspires holiest impulses. [E]very evening…the sun would go down, and crimson bannerets of clouds would follow in his royal wake. The tall grass would wave beneath the zephyr stealing up like a pet bird of stillest wing, from the twilight reaches of the dell beneath.*

The truth would be far less enchanting.

Miriam's journal revealed that she believed Clubb's stories, noting, "My husband has long been a practical vegetarian and we expect much from living in such a genial clime, where fruit is to quickly grown, and with people whose tastes and habits will coincide with our own."

For several weeks, the Colt family suffered the boredom and discomfort of train and wagon travel, arriving in St. Louis on April 22. Calling it "a city of smoke," Miriam went on to describe their lodgings: "Found ourselves in this miserable hotel before we knew it. Miserable fare—herring boiled with cabbage—miserable, dirty beds, and an odor pervading the house that is not at all agreeable." Moving on into the state, Miriam was impressed by the Missouri River scenery, although she began to get a sense of the Missouri weather: "The evening is dark; the thunder is roaring, the lightning flashing, and the rain comes in torrents. Here at

Jefferson City, have more of our company come on board. Good news from our southern home—our company happy and hopeful." The next day, April 27, the family passed the "pretty town of Booneville, where an old woman came on board to sell apples. The ship set off with her on it, and she was deposited four miles upstream on a bluff, to make her way home as best she could."

The trip to Kansas was difficult, with rains, floods and encounters with unfriendly locals and rattlesnakes. In the years before the Civil War, travel across Missouri was dangerous. Miriam described her father-in-law's encounter with border ruffians:

> *May 3.—Father, it seems, fell back a little and found a place to camp in a tavern where he fell in with the scores of Georgians who loaded a steamer and came up the river the same time that we did. He said he had to be very shrewd indeed not to have them find out that he was a "Free States" man. These Banditts have been sent in here, and will commit all sorts of depredations on the Free State settlers, and no doubt commit many a bloody murder.*

The company finally arrived at the "settlement" in early May, only to find that the promised land was wet, muddy and lacked any of the amenities promised by Clubb. Here were no water mills, schools, houses, agricultural college or "museum of curiosities and mechanic arts" but instead:

We leave our wagons and make our way to a large camp fire. Look about, and see the grounds all around the camp fire are covered with tents in which the families are staying. Not a house is to be seen. The ladies tell us they are sorry to see us come to this place; which plainly shows us that all is not right. No mills have been built...the directors, after receiving our money to build mills, have not fulfilled the trust reposed in them, and that, in consequence, some families have already left the settlement. As it is, we find the families, some living in tents of cloth, some of cloth and green bark just peeled from the trees, and some wholly of green bark, stuck upon the damp ground without floors or fires.

Miriam and William tried to settle in and enjoy the coming summer, with the promised heat, wildflowers and prairie grass. But the rainstorms were unbearable, and the lack of food and hygienic conditions took their toll on Miriam's spirit:

The dark storm-clouds, (to my mind's eye,) are gathering in our horizon, and even now they flap their cold, bat-like wings about my head, causing my heart to tremble with fear. I am so impressed some nights with this feeling, that I sit up in bed for hours, and fairly cringe from some unknown terror...I don't know why I should be so overpowered with such feelings; they

come to me without being invited, and I cannot help
giving them expression sometimes.

Miriam complained mightily about the mosquitoes,
noting that she could not sleep for their buzzing and
biting. Soon, the family came down with the "ague"—
malaria. William, Willie and Miriam shook with fever
and cold, unable to do a day's work when the attack was
upon them. She noted that Clubb had left the settlement
and that few families could expect to regain their
invested savings from him. The Colts struggled through
the summer, and to the misery of the ague were added
disabling attacks of dysentery. Finally, the family left for
Missouri in early September.

The return trip was filled with sickness and fear. At one
point, the teamster leading the Colts' wagon threatened
them with robbery, claiming he had become a border
ruffian. The family arrived in Boonville on September 20
and stayed at Bullock's hotel. By this time, Willie was very
ill, and the family's trunks had not arrived. Miriam made
do with whatever she had on hand; at one point, she was
shunned in the hotel dining room for wearing her bloomer
dress. Days were spent caring for her husband and son,
and a local doctor helped the family the best he could. On
the morning of September 24, Miriam soothed Willie as
he asked for white bread and apples and assumed that his
new appetite meant he was feeling better. Exhausted and
relieved, she napped but woke in a few minutes to find

FORGOTTEN TALES OF MISSOURI

that Willie had passed away in his sleep. "For while I slept, the angels came, and bore him away on their airy wings to their blissful bowers far beyond this scene of struggle… without waiting for him to receive father's, sisters or mother's kiss of adieu!"

Willie was buried in Sunset Hills, the old Boonville city burial ground, which still exists. Miriam described it as

> a lovely, retired, and shady spot, situated on a slowly-sloping hillside, with other hills rising higher all around, which nature had thickly set with trees, and in among were many large black walnuts, casting their large, lemon-shaped and colored nuts profusely to the ground. The rose, cypress, and myrtle interlaced over many a grave—the wind gently waved the drooping branches of the weeping willow, which bowed over the monuments in a mournful attitude, breathing a soothing requiem as they made up Willie's grave. We saw the little grave all filled up, evenly sodded over,—gazed upon it again and again; then gladly would I have lingered, but kind friends whispered, "your husband and little daughter are weak, and the night damp will soon begin to fall; come away." So we turned and left the spot, taking another glance, as we passed through the gate, and another as we were handed into the carriages, now bidding adieu, a last and long adieu, to the little mound where our Willie would sleep among strangers!

Miriam returned to town and began her search for a gravestone to stand guard over Willie. With little cash on hand, she decided to sell her extra clothing and use the money for the memorial. She walked down the street to Mr. Bedwell's stonemason shop.

> *Mr. Bedwell stood before me. I said, "I should like to get some small stones, if you will take some of my clothes which I do not need now"…At length he said, "I do not like to take a lady's clothing." I related the circumstances that compelled me to ask it, and assured him that he would confer a very great favor on me by so doing. He said he would call at the hotel and look at the clothes, and bade me select some stones, asking how I would have them lettered. I chose some that he would ask nine dollars for, and said "All I want marked on them is, Willie, the Little Stranger."*
>
> *He assured me that they should be immediately lettered, and if I did not leave to-day, might go out to the burying ground with him in the morning to see them set. I thanked him, returned to the hotel.*

Willie's death was announced in the *Boonville Weekly Observer*, noting, "In this city, on the 24th, Wm. H. Colt, Jr., aged 3 years and 8 months, son of W.H. Colt, of the State of New York." On September 26, Miriam had a strange dream in which she saw a black carriage carrying two people in black and two white sheep. She knew that the people were Mema and herself and that the sheep were Willie and his father. Knowing that her husband was very ill, Miriam asked him to pledge an unusual promise: "O, my own dear William, if there is any truth in the so-called 'spirit manifestations,' will you come to me?" William promised that if he could do so, he would. He died the next day, on October 3. Once again, the carriages and hearse made their trip to the burying grounds. Boonville people rallied around the family and made certain that Miriam was cared for. Women brought her proper mourning dress, housed her, paid for the funerals (including a twenty-dollar coffin, black velvet with silver-plated screws) and offered her their homes until she was well enough to travel. The townspeople offered her a governess's position, house, board and salary if she chose to live in Boonville. Once again, Miriam sold clothing to pay for the gravestone. William's obituary read: "DIED.—In this city, at even of the 3d inst., WM. H. COLT, son of John G. and Mary Colt, of the State of New York, aged 40 years, 3 months, and 3 days. The deceased leaves a wife and one little daughter to mourn his loss. As a husband, he was devotedly attached to his wife,—and a kind and indulgent father."

On October 19, Miriam Colt left Boonville, Missouri, to join friends in Michigan. She later learned that her in-laws—mother, sister and father—had perished as well in the Kansas experiment. In later years, Miriam bought a farm, raised her daughter and struggled to make ends meet.

She never gave up on her husband's promise and received "written notes" from spiritual mediums who copied down replies from "William" in the next world. In 1862, Miriam Davis Colt penned the classic *Went to Kansas*, which includes the story of her travails and losses. Willie and William still sleep peacefully together in Boonville.

Chapter 13

PRIVATE NEWCUM
AND THE LAND BOUNTY

*Your petitioner therefore prays, that your Honorable Bodies will
be pleased to grant such quantity of land and allow such pay
for the services aforesaid as to you may seem just and equitable,
and your petitioner as in duty bound will ever pray, etc.
—petition to Congress by Private Newcum*

By the 1840s, Native Americans had been pushed farther
and farther west, where the crush of tribes, horses,
ponies and mules was taking its toll on the land. Tribes found
it nearly impossible to maintain their traditional ways, food
was scarce and the poorly armed forts and supply trains
made appealing targets for Indian raids and attacks fueled
by desperation. Among the outposts set up to provide
security for troops and travelers was Fort Mann, located not
far from present-day Dodge City. The tiny fort, only about
2,200 square feet, consisted of four adobe buildings and
a stockade. Fort Mann was never given much support by

the military and from the start was understaffed and under constant attack and harassment from Comanche, Pawnee and other tribes. Finally, the United States government directed the army to form a battalion for the protection of the plains and the establishment of secure forts, including Fort Mann. The story of the battalion and two of its soldiers provides one of the more interesting tales about Missouri and the American military.

On September 17, 1847, Private Bill Newcum enrolled in Company D of the Indian Battalion Missouri Volunteers, which was under the command of Lieutenant Colonel William Gilpin. Gilpin was a soldier, lawyer, writer, speculator and land booster who fought in the Seminole Wars, accompanied John Fremont to the West and rejoined the army during the Mexican War. His battalion was given the job of securing the area around Fort Mann and Bent's Fort in Colorado. Although its mission was simple, the battalion itself was sometimes difficult to identify due to its many names, including the Battalion of Missouri Volunteers for the Plains, the Oregon Battalion, Gilpin's Battalion Missouri Mounted Volunteers, the Indian Battalion Missouri Volunteers and, finally, the Santa Fe Trace Battalion. It consisted of two mounted companies (A and B), an artillery company (C) and two infantry companies (D and E). Company D's membership included German immigrants from the St. Louis area, including the Schnabel brothers: Amandus, twenty-six, and Albert, eighteen. Their father, Ottomar, was a physician, and the brothers, along with their mother, brother and sister, joined Lutheran immigrants who set sail from Europe to settle in St. Louis. The voyage to New Orleans was difficult; of three ships that sailed together from Europe, only two made it to America.

After enrollment, Company D traveled from Missouri to Fort Leavenworth, where the soldiers spent a short time in training. The troops then set off on a thirty-day march to Fort Mann, where the three hundred soldiers of Companies C, D and E would winter.

Daily life for the Schnabels, Newcum and other soldiers can be deduced from the diary of James Bryant Hoover. A Missourian from Dallas County, Hoover was in mounted Company B and continued west to Bent's Fort. His diary noted that Gilpin's companies assembled in Buffalo, Missouri, near Springfield, where the men enjoyed a barbecue given by the county citizens. The battalion then marched for nine days to Fort Leavenworth and remained there until September 22, when they were sent to Fort Mann. For the next weeks, the soldiers marched up to twenty miles a day, hunted buffalo, endured bad water and wretched camping conditions and kept alert for Indian attacks. The untested troops must have found this world filled with wonders: "I gave this group of islands (Indian Island) this name because we found the remains of an Indian that had been raised some twenty feet into the top of a tree and snugly wrapped in a Buffalo skin," wrote Hoover. A few days later, "We saw a singular curiousity. That was the Cheyennes dragging their tent poles tied to their ponies and their dogs hauled their Buffalo meat."

Once settled in at Fort Mann, the soldiers drilled, gathered wood, repaired the fort and lived on limited rations. Given the fort's size, there were not enough buildings to accommodate the soldiers, and it appears many of them must have lived in tents throughout the cold season. The men spoke little English and had limited or no military experience. In the crowded conditions of the fort, tempers flared and discipline broke down quickly. Apparently, Amandus Schnabel was placed under arrest in October for attempting to remove an incompetent senior officer from command. Animals died from the cold, and soldiers suffered from illnesses, including scurvy. Gilpin purchased several tepees for his men (although it appears these were used by a company at Bent's Fort) and negotiated with the Cheyenne for buffalo meat. Hoover complained that "this substance resembled a parcel of raccoon skins thrown out in the back of a hatters shop." Because Amandus Schnabel was an officer, he may have had slightly better quarters than enlisted men like Newcum and Hoover. But records show that Newcum had been assigned work inside officers' quarters—especially those of Amandus Schnabel. For although the private was called William Newcum, in truth "he" was Elizabeth Caroline Newcum, a twenty-two-year-old Missouri adventuress.

Much of Elizabeth Newcum's life is hazy, including the spelling of her name, which was recorded variously as Newcum, Newcomb and Newcome. She gave her age at enlistment as twenty-two, making her birth year 1825, and while she lived in Missouri at the time of her enlistment, it is unclear whether she was born or raised in the state. Presumably, Elizabeth was unmarried at the time of her enlistment, but even that much is unknown. What is clear is that at some point she met and was wooed by Amandus V. Schnabel. From later military records, it appears that Schnabel convinced Elizabeth to pose as a man and enlist with him. There were few requirements for enlistment other than sound body, a somewhat sound mind and the ability to learn basic skills like marksmanship, marching and drill. Apparently, Elizabeth was able to fool the commanding officers, but there can be little doubt that in the close quarters of Fort Mann her fellow soldiers were aware of her gender.

Elizabeth must have been a young woman of grit, since as an infantryman she traveled from St. Louis to Fort Mann camping and enduring difficult living conditions. She served for ten months in the unit, but by May 1848, Elizabeth was pregnant. One story claimed that Amandus encouraged her to desert by hiding in a wagon heading back to Missouri, but Elizabeth changed her mind, returned to her unit and confessed. She was discharged at Fort Leavenworth, having been "discovered to be a disguised woman," while Amandus was court-martialed for his role in the deception, partly on the grounds that he denied the military the services of a soldier. He returned to St. Louis and his family, and little was heard of him in later years, although he apparently married Martha A. Stewart in St. Louis in 1856 when he was thirty-five.

Elizabeth appears to have moved to the western part of Missouri and married. But her five years away from the military did little to quench her spirit. In 1853, Mrs. Elizabeth (Newcum) Smith filed a claim in Platte County, Missouri, for back pay and the 160 acres of bounty land due to soldiers who served in the Mexican War. She stated that under

> *the assumed name of "Bill Newcume,"…she wore the uniform dress of a soldier, was to receive the same pay as such, that she served her Government faithfully and honestly, for the space of ten months or about that length of time when she was discharged from the Army of the United States, at Fort Leavenworth, the place of enlistment, to wit: on or about the fifteenth day of June, AD 1848, by reason of the discovery before that time made that she was not "Bill or William Newcume" the person represented on the Muster Roll but that she was Elizabeth Caroline Newcume a female instead of a male and therefore was discharged.*

Despite her relationship with Amandus, Elizabeth swore that

> *she enlisted from the best of motives, that of serving her country, that she did serve as long as she was permitted to for which she has never been remunerated by the Government in any way, and that she makes this application in order to obtain a Bounty-Land Warrant for 160 acres of land. She further declares that she served under the circumstances and in the manner as herein set forth, that she is now the lawful wife of John Smith and resides in the County of Platte and State of Missouri.*

Her case must have surprised Congress—while women had participated in warfare during settlement times, she was the first woman to have served as a solider west of the Mississippi. After reviewing the documents, including affidavits from a soldier who served with Elizabeth, Congress agreed to pass a special bill:

> *There seems to be no doubt that the service was rendered as charged, and that she is entitled to her pay for the same, as the law makes no distinction with regard to sex; and as her services were as useful to the government as if she had been a man, and regularly enlisted as such. The committee, considering her fully entitled to regular pay for her services, as well as three months'*

extra pay, under the fifth section of the act approved 19th July, 1848, and to bounty land, under the ninth section of the act approved February 11, 1847, beg leave to report a bill for her relief.

Mrs. Smith apparently returned to Missouri, where she lived out her remaining days, only the second woman granted a military pension and perhaps the only female soldier to travel the Santa Fe Trail. Elizabeth Newcum defied convention, followed her heart and refused to be considered anything less than a patriot and a soldier.

Chapter 14

WIND WAGONS WEST

Missouri was the perfect jumping-off point in the 1840s for migrants heading to Oregon, California, Colorado and other points west. But while adventure and hope for new opportunities drove the traveler, the travel itself was time-consuming and tedious. Wagons and oxen were costly to own, maintain and repair, while Missouri mules earned their reputation for orneriness by kicking, biting and just plain not moving. Railroads were in the future, horses were impractical on many trails and to head west by water meant crossing the Isthmus of Panama, an often stomach-churning sea journey and land crossing. But some men had a vision for a new method of transportation using free, unlimited and clean fuel that Missouri could provide all year-round.

In December 1846, the *Independence Expositor* announced: "The Wind Wagon Works. Mr. Thomas ran up and down the plains with his wagon at pleasure. It is his intention to move his family to Independence and with a partner (an old tar) begin a shipping business to Santa Fe in a reasonable time at $6 per hundred pounds." This was apparently the first time a Missouri newspaper reported on the wind wagon, brainchild of adventurer and inventor William "Windwagon" Thomas. Using wind to propel a land vehicle was not a new idea: ancient cultures, including Egypt and China, developed land ships, sailing wagons and wind wagons, variations on what today are called land yachts. European travelers to seventeenth-century Holland described the vehicles, and Dutch artists depicted wind wagons on pottery and in paintings. Maurice of Nassau, Prince of Orange, commissioned the design and construction of two wind wagons so that he might entertain his guests along the seashore. A contemporary print shows two large wagons with sails and iron-bound, wide wheels suitable for driving over the sand.

A wind wagon was fitted out with canvas or linen sails and ship's rigging, and the pilot navigated the vehicle with a tiller. The vehicles worked best in areas with constant wind: near the ocean, on salt flats and in the plains region of the great West. How or where Thomas got the idea for his wind wagon is not known, but as early as 1846, he was at work near Independence, Missouri. Thomas had a grand plan for his invention: he hoped to create a transcontinental service that could move people and goods from the East Coast to the West in affordable comfort. He had a well thought-out plan, with "cars" on either side of rivers, ready to load passengers and freight and then sweep them across the prairies to California, Oregon country and the trading center of Santa Fe. The *Independence Expositor* described the vehicle in detail:

> *The construction of the wagon is very simple. It is a frame made of plank, well braced and placed edgewise on four axle-trees, four wheels to each side, these wheels to be 12 feet or more in diameter and one foot broad. Two tongues are joined together forward of the wagon and by ropes coming to the wheel similar to the pilot wheel of a steamboat, the wagon is steered by a pilot. The sails are like to the sails and rigging of a ship. Mr. Thomas expects to convey freight and passengers.*

In order to advance his dream, Thomas founded the Overland Navigation Company in 1853 and convinced some investors to back it. No one is certain where the wind wagon was built; some point to the Robison and Crook Foundry in Independence, while others claim that Fritz Lauber of Westport did the work. From descriptions and a few illustrations, apparently the large wheels lifted the wagon bed over any obstacles, and passengers could see for miles across the prairie. In some cases, the vehicle was steered by heading the rear of the wagon into the wind and pulling the wagon tongue up to use like a rudder.

According to historian Stanley Vestal, there was more to Windwagon Thomas than met the eye. Vestal claimed

that Thomas may have been a Yankee seafarer, that he convinced investors to join him by sailing a small wagon to Council Grove and back to Independence in nine days and that the local Missouri backers included Dr. J.W. Parker, Indian agent Benjamin Newson, lawyer J.J. Mastin, Henry Sager and Thomas W. Adams. Vestal described the wagon as twenty-five feet long, with a mainsail and a deck. For the wagon's maiden voyage, Thomas, accompanied by curious townspeople and the investors, had the wagon rafted across the Missouri River and then towed by oxen to the Kansas prairies. The investors, if the story is to be believed, climbed "below decks" into the wagon, Thomas adjusted the sails and the wind wagon caught at the breeze and then took off across the grasslands, bumping and rocking and gathering speed. All went well at first, until the wagon began to run ahead of the wind, much faster than anyone on board had ever traveled. Dr. Parker, sensing possible disaster, chased the vehicle on his mule and was nearly run down. The investors waited as long as they could until, terrified, they finally jumped into the grass. Thomas stayed aboard, trying to maintain control, but the wagon ran into a dry stream bed, spun around and smashed against a fence. The bruised and battered investors refused to give Thomas a penny more, and his dreams of prairie domination were gone with the breezes.

Although looked upon as novelties today, the wind wagons were actively used by travelers on the plains, and at least two other Missouri inventors, August Rodert and Dr.

John Parker, continued the wind wagon saga. Rodert was a German immigrant living in Westport, where he founded the Great Western Wagon Works in 1857. Rodert's wagon used a small windmill to power the vehicle. Parker (who saw the first wind wagon attempt) designed and built a wagon with a mast and four cross-arms. The front and rear axles were steered separately by men who stood in the wagon. It was a large vehicle, at least twenty feet in length and four feet wide, and brightly painted. According to one story, Parker's wagon was pulled to the prairie by oxen (mules refused to go near it). The wagon was left there overnight, and in the morning, it was gone. It was never found, and folks believed it was sailing the prairies under its own steam. Another story told how Parker used his "sailing wagon" to visit his patients.

Perhaps the most successful captain was Samuel Peppard of Kansas, who built a wind wagon in the 1860s that traveled fast enough to pass migrant wagons heading to Pike's Peak. A newspaperman writing for *Leslie's Illustrated Magazine* reported the arrival of

> the *Wind Ship of the Prairies: Fort Kearney, May 27, 1860. The prairie ship,...is a very light built wagon, the body rounded in front, something in shape like a boat. The wheels are remarkably light, large and slender, and the whole vehicle strongly built. Two masts...carry large square sails, rigged like a ship's. In front is a large coach lamp, to travel by night when the*

wind is favorable…The ship hove in sight about eight o'clock in the morning, with a fresh breeze from N.E. by E.; it was running down in a westerly direction for the fort, under full sail across the green prairie. The guard, astonished at such a novel sight, reported the matter to the officer on duty, and we all turned out to view the phenomenon.

Outside of Denver, the wagon was picked up by a "whirlwind" and dropped to the ground. (Other stories were less dramatic, reporting that the wind wagon blew into a ravine and was smashed.) Eventually, railroads eliminated the need for oxen, mules and wind wagons, although John Wornall of Westport was using a wagon as late as 1887 for trips to camp meetings. In a state where tall tales are called "windies," the Missouri wind wagons still sail the prairies of imagination.

Chapter 15

The Todds of Missouri

Missouri was a microcosm of the United States during the Civil War, divided as it was between pro- and antislavery factions. Settled by a volatile mix of people from the South, the Northeast and overseas, the state was rent by vicious partisanships that used murder and physical intimidation to support their beliefs. Even Abraham Lincoln rarely visited the state, which voted for Stephan A. Douglas in the 1860 election. But another Lincoln spent time in Missouri as a young woman, and her familial relations there played an important but forgotten role in the state's story.

The Todd family arrived in Missouri during early statehood, when attorney David Todd settled in Franklin. Todd was a well-liked, popular man who ran for public office and was later appointed to the judicial bench. Judge Todd had many friends in the law, among them Peyton Hayden. Although Todd and Hayden were on opposite sides in many court cases, the men remained close friends throughout their lives. They traveled the judicial circuit throughout Missouri, and in order to pass the time, they would play elaborate practical jokes on each other. Under the rules of this game, the first man to complain about the joke was fined money, liquor or both. One night, Judge Todd and his friends were in Liberty, Missouri, on their way to a hotel kept by a "buxom widow" who was fond of Judge Todd and invariably gave him the most comfortable room in the place. The attorneys were determined to deprive Todd of the luxuries, so they rode ahead, leaving behind Todd and Hayden to catch up. Hayden was a sweet-faced man who wore his hair in the old-fashioned, long style, pulled back behind his head and held in place with a comb. When the jokester attorneys arrived at the widow's house, she asked after Todd. His "friends," knowing the upright and moral character of the widow, hinted that Todd had fallen from the righteous path and was traveling with a woman not his wife who was dressed as a man. The widow was horrified—she had always treated the judge with respect, and this is what he brought to her house! Just then, Todd and the unsuspecting Hayden arrived, and the widow, "her tongue fast and loose at both ends," screamed at Hayden, "You vile wretch. You nasty, stinking hussy, dressed in men's clothes and running around the country with judges and lawyers. You are a shame and a disgrace to your sex. Leave here, both of

you! You shan't pollute my house with your presence!"
Judge Todd and his "paramour," poor Hayden, had to
ride back ten miles to another hotel.

In June 1840, David Todd and his brother, North,
attended the Whig convention in Rocheport (William

Henry Harrison and John Tyler were the presidential candidates). The event was a popular gathering for men and women interested in politics, so the brothers were happy to escort their pretty niece, Mary Todd. Mary was visiting her Columbia relations, including cousins Robert L. and Robert B. Todd. Although often portrayed as a woman with little sense, in fact, Mary Todd loved politics and enjoyed debates. She certainly was not a prude, as shown by her attendance at the convention. From June 18 to 20, between six and ten thousand people made their way to the tiny river town of Rocheport. The gathering was held on a hill east of town, "in a dense grove of sugar trees." Tents, camps and covered wagons were everywhere. Three speaker's stands were set up, and day and night speeches were declaimed, along with many toasts of hard cider. Some men came in coonskin caps, buckskin and other reminders of their frontier past. There were parades, an old soldiers' convention and a Young Men's Day, at which Missourians George Caleb Bingham, James S. Rollins and A. Doniphan spoke. The opposition press sneered at the "whiglings" and "ciderites," but all agreed that the gathering offered much in the way of speeches, parades and good Missouri liquor. Mary felt right at home among the roistering.

According to family stories that circulated years later, Mary may have spied among the multitudes one of her beaus: gawky, brilliant lawyer Abe Lincoln. It is possible that Lincoln had been traveling the court circuit from Illinois to Missouri, stopped in St. Louis and decided to join the official Missouri Whig delegation on its steamboat journey to Rocheport. (Besides his court and election work, Lincoln had recently attended the Whig National Convention in Illinois on June 3 and 4.) As an unofficial member of the Missouri delegation, he would not be listed in the official documents of the convention and apparently was not invited to speak. Some historians claim that Lincoln did not attend the convention. But a Todd family story said that Abe later caught a steamboat to Providence, a tiny river town now all but forgotten, and walked several miles into Columbia, where he visited the Todds and Mary. Abe and Mary had been courting, and she hints in a July 23, 1840 letter to friend and confidante Mercy Levering that she has been receiving "unlooked for" letters and might have a decision to make, commenting that she expected to marry for love and to live a quiet life. (She did, indeed, accept a proposal from Abe in late summer, although the couple later broke off their engagement before finally marrying in 1842.)

Abe would have met Mary's cousins, Robert Levi (Little Bob Todd) and Robert Barr Todd (Big Bob Todd). The young men were later the first graduates of the University of Missouri in 1843, with Little Bob as valedictorian and Big Bob as salutatorian. (Neither received their diplomas for two years, when the university caught up with issuing the documents.) Robert Levi remained close to the University of Missouri, serving as a tutor, curator and booster for the school. But according to Judge Richard Gentry in a 1913 article, Todd should also be called "hero" at the university today. Gentry told the story set in August 1862:

> *Two hundred confederate soldiers dashed into Columbia at about two p.m., and stationed guards at the crossings of Broadway and 6th, 7th, 8th, 9th and 10th streets, while most of the soldiers visited the county jail to release prisoners. The federal soldiers were completely taken by surprise. After the battle was over, the federal commander (Col. Lewis Merrill) was very angry and said that some Columbia citizens had informed the enemy that no sentinels or pickets were on duty (which probably was true), and he intended to retaliate by burning the town and the university building. Several union men of Columbia tried to dissuade him from such an unwise course, but he said he had determined to do so, and would do so at once. Then Mr. Robert L. Todd went to see him, and after talking pleasantly for a few minutes, with no success, Mr. Todd said, "Well, sir, you are to blame for this whole business; you should have had guards out on every road leading into Columbia, and most every other military man in the country would have done so. You have other duties besides speaking on the occasion of a flag presentation. Now, sir, if you set fire to and burn our town and our university, the friends of our town and of our university will kindle a fire under*

*you, and I tremble for you at the result." This ended
all talk about burning the town or the university. As
a result of the occupancy of the university grounds
and buildings by federal soldiers, the buildings were
damaged in various ways; and many years after that
congress appropriated Five thousand dollars to pay
for such damages. This money was accepted by the
university authorities, and the same was used to pay
for the erection of the stone entrance to the campus at
the South end of eight street.*

There is a footnote to this standoff: Merrill's men
camped on the university grounds, and he used the
university president's residence as his headquarters.
Merrill was a proud and stubborn man, and he would
not have taken lightly Robert Todd's snub. Mary Todd
might have been first lady, but she was a Southerner, and
a Todd Columbia cousin was fighting for the South. On
November 28, 1865, the residence burned to the ground,
and two weeks later, Merrill left the military, leaving
behind a tantalizing mystery as to the fire's origin.

Mary Lincoln never returned to Missouri, but her
family remained there and helped shape the University of
Missouri. Visitors to Columbia may still visit the Todds,
now located at the Columbia Cemetery on Broadway,
where they rest in peace not far from their old homes and a
university they loved.

Chapter 16

THE LONG BLACK VEIL

The horrors of slavery and civil war need little description here, and there is no justification for ownership of one human by another. But often buried in the sweeping histories of the war are the stories of the average person: the uncle murdered by bushwhackers, sons fighting against each other, the loss of everything to marauders who raided both sides. The Missouri Daughters of the Confederacy began collecting stories from their members in the first decade of the twentieth century, fearful that the memories, experiences and opinions of the Southern woman would be forgotten as the war generation faded away. The following story was related by Mrs. Alexander H. Major of Saint Louis, and though it is unclear where the tragedy unfolded, the despair was universal.

Mrs. Major had lived in Missouri and eastern Kansas and her father was a Southern man, but her husband served under General William Tecumseh Sherman. In

1865, she followed the Union troops to an unidentified town. Most Confederate families had fled except for a Mrs. Stuart, who refused to leave her home until she was carried out "feet foremost." The Majors boarded with Mrs. Stuart, who seemed to accept Mrs. Major's Southern roots even if she was traveling with the Yankees. Mrs. Stuart's story was not unusual for the war: her husband died at Antietam and her son, a drummer boy, died with Stonewall Jackson's troops. "I hate the Yanks, I will never forgive Lincoln for having brought on this terrible war," she told Mrs. Major. "I wear black for my dead and I weep, but if anything happened to Lincoln, I would be tempted to flaunt the gaudiest colors I could."

Mrs. Stuart got her wish, since within days a courier brought news that Lincoln had been shot at Ford's Theatre. "Thank God," cried Mrs. Stuart at her front gate, "the wretch has gotten his just desserts." The Union courier warned Mrs. Stuart to watch her tongue. A day later, Lincoln's death was confirmed, and all the families in town were ordered to drape their houses in mourning black. Young bullies and ruffians patrolled the streets making certain the order was carried out. They stopped at Mrs. Stuart's home and, knowing of her comments, demanded that she not only drape the house in black but that she use something of her own, shouting, "Every damned Rebel must this day kiss the dust for this dastardly act." Pushing their way inside, the young men ransacked the house and found Mrs. Stuart's mourning veil, which was sacred to the memory of her husband and son. They demanded that she hang the veil from the house in memory of Lincoln. Mrs. Major intervened and begged the young men to let her use other black fabric that would do as well, but they ignored her and continued their demands. Mrs. Stuart stood quietly and listened and then agreed to hang the veil but asked the boys and Mrs. Major to leave the house and wait out front while she accomplished the task.

Mrs. Major wrote, "She came out on the veranda. I noticed she had changed her dress since we had come away, and had the veil wound once around her neck." Mrs. Stuart stood on a chair, carefully tied the veil to the edge of the veranda—and then, to everyone's horror, jumped from her chair and over the railing. All rushed to her aid, but it was too late: beneath the veil was found a stout rope. Mrs. Stuart had joined her loved ones.

Chapter 17

Frankie, Albert and Stagger Lee

At the turn of the twentieth century, St. Louis was home to districts famous for their nightlife, honkytonks, crime and great music. Scott Joplin, Tom Turpin and John "Blind" Boone played in Chestnut Valley (near Market and Chestnut Streets), where ragtime music was birthed and the blues reached adulthood. The districts were generally poor and overcrowded, home to men and women forced into the areas by restrictive race laws. As with any city, murder and crime bellied up to the bars and dives, and the lurid events were forgotten as quickly as the next newspaper edition was printed. But once in a while, the stories hit a nerve with those musicians who sang about the down and out, the poor, those suffering from the blues. Two of those songs became St. Louis legends and remain unforgettable generations later.

FRANKIE AND ALBERT

Frankie went to the barroom
Ordered her a glass of brew.
Says to the bartender,
"Has my lovin' man been here?"
He's my man,
But he's doin' me wrong.

On October 19, 1899, seventeen-year-old Allen "Albert" Britt died at the St. Louis City Hospital. His death was only one of a half dozen or more that night, but what set Britt's passing apart from the other deceased was his method of dying: he was shot by his older girlfriend, Frankie Baker. She was twenty-four at the time, a working girl, a slight, beautiful woman despite the razor scar bestowed upon her by a rival. Known as a flashy dresser, Frankie enjoyed the good life, including diamonds "as big as hens' eggs," flowers and fashionable gowns. But the word on the street was that Frankie could and would defend herself: she was dangerous when riled but a "queen sport" when having a good time. Boyfriend Albert Britt was born in Kentucky and moved to St. Louis with his parents. He was a musician who played in the bars and a sporting man who set up his gal with appointments. It was said that Frankie and Albert met and fell in love instantly at the Orange Blossoms Hall, a dance palace and saloon. They quickly became lovers and moved in together at 212 Targee Street, continuing their individual lines of work and hilarity.

Frankie doted on Albert and was openhanded with her earnings, buying him clothing, meals and gifts. But spoiled and pampered, Albert gave little thought to the consequences of toying with a woman's affections, especially one as strong-minded and independent as Frankie. On the evening of October 15, Albert Britt made the terrible mistake of stepping out with Alice Pryor, another lady of the evening, while Frankie was entertaining a client. The seemingly carefree couple spent the evening at Stolle's Dance Hall (some sources said the Phoenix Hotel), joining the cakewalk and winning the dance competition, in which intricate footwork won a prize cake and cash. According to one story, Frankie appeared at the hall and began a fight with Albert, who refused to leave. Frankie stomped out, leaving behind a shaken Alice and a defiant Albert, who spent the night with his new love. He returned in the wee hours to the Targee house, where Frankie waited and the argument continued. Finally, Frankie screamed that she was going to find Alice and presumably take care of her, and Albert threatened to kill Frankie if she left. Although one newspaper reported that Frankie was armed with a knife, in truth she took aim with a pistol and fired at Albert, the bullet passing through his gut. Albert was taken to the hospital, and Frankie "escaped" but was reported locked up by October 19, the day Albert expired from his wound.

A coroner's jury hauled Frankie into court, where she and her girlfriend Pansy Marvin testified to the events of October 15. Pansy, who may or may not have been in the Targee Street house, said she saw Albert pull out a knife and take a swipe at Frankie, who yelled, "Don't you cut me!" Frankie then stepped back, pulled out a pistol from under her bed pillow and shot Albert. He staggered away, but Frankie stood there, afraid that he was faking his injury, trying to draw her closer so he could stab her. Despite the wound, Albert dragged himself to his mother's house down the road, and she called the police. Although Albert lived long enough to identify Frankie as his killer, the law saw things differently. On November 13, Frankie told the jury that she "didn't shoot but one time. Standing by the bed." She also said that Albert had beaten her several days before and that he had attacked her again that night with a lamp, yelling that he was the boss and was going to protect himself. Frankie was acquitted of murder and released on Friday the thirteenth, a lucky day for her; the police even returned her gun. Albert was buried in St. Peter's Cemetery, St. Louis, in an unmarked grave.

Less than two weeks after Albert's death, a song was heard in the beer joints of St. Louis. Said to have been composed by singer Bill (or Jim) Dooley, the ballad was called "Frankie Killed Allen" and was a thinly disguised version of the killing. One story says that Albert's father was horrified that his son's name was associated with the song and demanded that Dooley change it, which Dooley did, choosing the less obvious Johnny.

> *Frankie went by the house.*
> *She did not give no 'larm,*
> *She looked in through the window glass*
> *And saw Albert in the woman's arms*
> *He was her man, Lawd,*
> *Doin' her wrong.*

But while Albert was soon forgotten, Frankie's problems were just beginning. She left St. Louis soon after the trial, first moving to Ohio and later to Oregon because she had read about the roses there. Frankie was a working girl and then opened a shoeshine parlor and later was a chambermaid at the Royal Palm Hotel, all the while trying to remain anonymous. "Frankie and Johnny" had by then become a standard and was sung by performers all over the country, but Frankie avoided publicity until 1933. That was when Mae West and Cary Grant appeared in the film *She Done Him Wrong*, which included a sexy version of "Frankie and Johnny." The film pulled Frankie into the center of journalistic attention. "I just want to be left alone," she told an interviewer. "I can't even leave my house. If people had left me alone, I'd have forgotten this thing a long time ago." At the time, she was living in Portland at 22 North Clackamas Street, in a small wooden house with a garden. Ill and nearly broke,

Frankie finally sued the film studios for $200,000 over the West film, as well as *Frankie & Johnny*, which had also been released. During the trial, music historian Sigmund Spaeth appeared as an expert witness for the film studios and lied about the song's origins while under oath; he had once championed Albert's murder as the song's inspiration but reversed himself on the stand. Frankie was accused of trying to make a fortune "because forty years ago she shot a little boy here in St. Louis." The all-white, all-male jury found for the defendant. Frankie now had more publicity than ever and returned home to deal with her notoriety and poverty the best she could.

In March 1950, a judge committed an elderly woman to a Pendleton, Oregon mental asylum. She was suffering from dementia and deemed a danger to herself and others. Frankie Baker died there two years later, poor and elderly but still the queen of her district, at least in the words and lyrics.

> *It was not murder in the first degree*
> *Nor murder in the third,*
> *A woman simply dropped her man,*
> *Like a hunter dropped a bird.*
> *She shot her man*
> *For doin' her wrong.*

STAGGER LEE

If Frankie Baker was a real woman trapped in a story that took over her life, then Stagger Lee was her male counterpart. Known variously as Stagger Lee, Stagolee and Stackolee, his real name may have been Lee Shelton. Whether he picked up his nickname along the Mississippi riverfront or from the shipping company of Stacker Lee, or whether he gained it because he was a "stag," or a sporting man, is unknown, but time and balladry assigned many stories to him. Lee lived in St. Louis at North Twelfth Street, worked as a carriage driver and was very, very tough. Among his most distinguishing sartorial features was his black Stetson hat, a mark of style in the St. Louis bawdy district and regions around. It was this hat that launched the legend.

On Christmas Day 1895, William "Billy" Lyons, a worker on the steamboat levees, stopped at Curtis's Saloon on Thirteenth and Morgan for some gambling and drinking. The bar was a rough-and-tumble dive where prostitution and gambling were available and violence was only a breath away. Lyons saw Lee there, and the two men drank together until trouble erupted. No one knows whether the problem was a game of dice or an argument over politics, but Lee pulled off Lyon's derby and crushed it. Lyon demanded payment for the hat and then snatched the Stetson from Lee. The men argued, and Lee threatened to kill Lyons. Lee reached for his gun, and Lyons pulled a knife and advanced on his opponent. Lee fired, hitting Lyons in the abdomen, and then took his hat from the dying man's hand and walking out of the bar without a backward glance. Lee went home, gave the gun to his girlfriend and took a nap. Lyons died the next day, and Lee was arrested soon after and held at the Chestnut Street Station in St. Louis on a charge of first-degree murder. His first trial ended in no decision, and a retrial was ordered. This time, the cards were stacked against Lee, and he was sent to the Missouri State Penitentiary in Jefferson City on October 7, 1897.

While in prison, Lee was whipped for idleness and later provided information to prison guards. He lived in the A Hall, but political pressure from friends and connections resulted in a 1909 pardon. Although ill with tuberculosis, he resumed his old life, committing assault and armed robbery. Returned to prison, he died there in 1912 at age forty-seven and is buried in Greenwood Cemetery in Hillsdale, Missouri.

Shelton's story entered popular culture immediately. The trials were covered in detail by the St. Louis newspapers, and off-color, violent lyrics retold the story again and again. Folklorists would later collect stories about "Stackalee" that said that he made a deal with the devil: as long as Stackalee wore his hat, he could get away with anything. But once it was stolen, Stackalee would lose his powers. So when Billy Lyons stole the hat, Stackalee lost his mind. Later, the devil was so scared of Stack that he sent him back to earth so Stack could serve his prison time instead and leave hell alone.

> *Everybody's talkin 'bout Stackalee*
> *that bad man Stackalee,*
> *Oh, tough man Stackalee.*
> *Oh, oh, Lord, Lord, Lord,*
> *All about an old Stetson hat.*

Chapter 18

BEATEN BISCUITS BUILD A FORTUNE

In a 1919 speech, entrepreneur Annie Fisher called herself a fifty-seven-year-old woman not afraid to tell her age. A hardworking, no-nonsense lady, Mrs. Fisher was known to one and all as Annie. She was wealthy, had a nationally renowned catering company and had fed the rich and famous on Missouri ham and beaten biscuits—a business triumph for any woman at the time but an amazing story for a black woman descended from slaves.

Annie Fisher was born on December 3, 1867, to Charlotte and Robert Knowles, slaves of the Bouchelle family in Boone County, Missouri. Few records remain of Annie's childhood, but she described her life in a speech before the National Negro Business League in 1919. While still a child herself, Annie was sent out into the world to earn money by rocking cradles for white infants and helping with general child care. Her own family was quite large, and her father, Robert Knowles, struggled to provide for his wife and children.

Annie described a difficult life but one common among the African American community. When she was done caring for the children, she was encouraged to "be industrious" and sent to the kitchen to help the cook. There, Annie began to learn the basics of what would become a lifelong art. "I was always fond of cooking," she recalled, "and the cook would sometimes give me some dough to make up which I would roll out and make into biscuits; sometimes they were not altogether right, and no matter if, at times, they were only half-baked, I enjoyed them very much, for those biscuits were the product of my own hands."

By the time she was a teenager, Annie was "working out" for white families in Columbia. She was paid very little but received castoff clothing as part of her "benefits." "Most that I got for as the result of my labor was a few old clothes formerly worn by the white people where I worked," she recalled, "and at that time, was very glad to get them for I couldn't afford to buy new ones." Annie made do the best she could but recalled a particularly stinging comment made by an older woman in her church. Annie attended services in an "old second-hand party costume that was five or ten years out of date" when the congregant shouted out, "Good Lord, move back and give Annie Fisher plenty of room for here she comes dressed like a peacock, and she ought to know that the house of the Lord isn't the place for any such clothes as them." True to her spirit, Annie sat through the church services with her head held high.

Annie worked during her teenage years to help her family, but as her brothers and sisters grew old enough to care for themselves, she began to save for her own home. By her early twenties, she had purchased a tiny, two-room house and was cooking and baking for the wealthy city families of Columbia, as well as the Sigma Alpha Epsilon fraternity house. Annie married and had a daughter, Lucile. During this time, one of Annie's employers suggested that she branch out into catering, which would provide her with a better living. Annie took the advice to heart and began to bake cakes and biscuits and make salads for dinners and parties, building on her connections with society matrons and church ladies. The business took off quickly, buoyed by Annie's reputation and skill, and she was proud to tell businesspeople that while it took her five years to save for a down payment, she paid off the house less than two years after she went into business.

Of all her recipes, Annie was best known for her beaten biscuits, a traditional southern recipe in which the dough was "raised" by folding and beating it to create air pockets, a process that could take more than an hour. Beaten biscuits were usually whacked hundreds of times with a rolling pin, although some stories claim that axe handles, irons or other heavy implements would do as well. Annie probably first resorted to a rolling pin but later in life may have used a "biscuit brake," a kitchen contraption with rollers and handles that let the cook avoid much of the pounding.

Annie's beaten biscuits gained national prominence, and she won an award for her baking at the 1904 St. Louis World's Fair. Among her specialties were fruit cake, "chipped" potatoes, roast chicken and ice cream. Annie was proud of cooking in what she called "old Missouri style," which meant cooking from scratch with local ingredients. She always offered to return a client's money if he was not pleased, noting, "I have never had to return any money yet." In the days before kitchen mechanization, Annie peeled, beat and baked everything by hand. Although she catered for small parties, she was the main caterer for events at local universities, banquets and other large celebrations. It was nothing for her to bake 1,200 biscuits or serve more than five hundred people a full dinner. Annie maintained her own supplies of china and silverware, which represented a substantial investment on her part. She was famous across the state for both her cooking and her business acumen. Once, when a university refused to lend her silverware for an event, Annie headed into St. Louis, borrowed the silverware from another restaurant and later returned every piece. She would earn over $1,000 for some events, an enormous sum in the early twentieth century.

Annie always remembered her childhood spent in poverty and decided early on to invest in real estate.

From that simple two-room house, Annie went on to own a fourteen-room city home, eighteen rental houses, a catering establishment and a fifty-eight-acre farm outside the city where she raised hogs, cows and crops for her cooking. Her business was not limited to Missouri, however, as she built up a successful mail-order business in biscuits and fruitcakes. She was often invited to cater large events out of state and rented out her catering equipment and dinnerware to other groups when not in use.

Annie died in 1938 at the age of seventy from heart problems. Her death certificate noted that she was a cook, divorced and "of the colored race." She was a successful businesswoman who had only a basic education, a community leader born to slaves and a cook who rarely had a solid meal as a child. Annie Fisher summed up her philosophy in a newspaper interview in 1911: "I can tell you how to write a menu for any occasion, but I surely can't tell you much about myself."

Chapter 19

SCOTT JOPLIN'S TRUNK

For nearly 150 years, the sound of ragtime has flowed through Missouri, a music born, bred and brought to a syncopated sophisticated adulthood there. Ragtime came from the bordellos, streets and elegant private clubs where the finger-busting works of John "Blind" Boone and the melodies of Scott Joplin, Arthur Marshall and others made feet tap and spines snap to rhythms heard nowhere else. While ragtime had many fathers—sliding rhythms and beats from Africa and, some say, Ireland, risqué sounds and lyrics from work camps, red-light districts, a touch or two from the formal classics—it had only one mother, Missouri, and among her adopted sons was Scott Joplin. He was the Entertainer in the flesh and made Missouri his home, where he envisioned new genres: ragtime ballets, folk operas and other celebrations. His life was a legend within legend, for he left behind a mystery still mused over in Missouri's ragtime retreats.

Joplin was born in Texas around 1867, son of a former slave and a free woman of color. Details vary about Joplin's early life, but he received musical training and his mother exposed him to classical music and opera. Joplin's mother worked for the white families of their town, and it is possible that Scott had access to a piano at their houses. As a young man, Joplin worked as a traveling musician on violin, piano and cornet. He was also a singer, performing at minstrel shows, concerts and whatever other venues would hire black musicians and entertainers. By the early 1880s, Joplin had appeared at Tom Turpin's St. Louis saloon, the Silver Dollar, and had gained recognition as a fine musician. (Turpin cast a large shadow in the history of ragtime, both figuratively and literally. A big man, over three hundred pounds, he ran saloons, served as a political leader and was the first composer to publish a ragtime tune.)

Joplin returned to Sedalia in the mid-1890s, where he studied music at George R. Smith College, a school for black students. It was in Sedalia that Joplin assumed his nickname (and the title of one of his most famous works), "The Entertainer." He played at the Maple Leaf Club, Wood's Opera House and the Black 400 Club. Sedalia is where Joplin composed "The Maple Leaf Rag," among the most famous ragtime pieces. The tune's royalties provided Joplin with some financial security, allowing him to expand his compositional work to longer, more "serious" works. While Joplin became known as the

"King of Ragtime," he was also determined to write new classics. In the early twentieth century, he wrote a ballet and two operas, including *Treemonisha*, about a young woman who overcomes the power of conjuration and magic to teach her people that education was a stronger force in life. (*Treemonisha* did not receive a full production during Joplin's lifetime, but it was revived in the early 1970s and contributed to Joplin's posthumous Pulitzer Prize in music.)

Although there are mysteries about Joplin's life, perhaps the most intriguing one involved a trunk filled with manuscripts, a debt and a missing opera. Between 1901 and 1903, Joplin conceived, composed and presented the opera *A Guest of Honor* to audiences throughout the Midwest. The opera's subject matter was astonishing for the time. Joplin took as his story the recent (1901) visit of Booker T. Washington to a White House dinner with President Theodore Roosevelt. Washington was the head of Tuskegee Institute in Alabama. His autobiography, *Up from Slavery*, had captured the attention of the general public, and Roosevelt was a man interested in the future of all Americans. According to the *Atlanta Constitution*, at 8:00 p.m. on October 16, Booker Washington, "the well known negro educator, president of the Tuskegee, Ala. Institute," presented himself at the White House at the invitation of President Theodore Roosevelt. Although there is no record of what occurred during the evening, the usual tradition at informal dinners with the Roosevelts

was for guests to dine with the family and then for the president and his guest to enjoy an after-dinner chat and presumably drinks or a cigar in the library. Washington left the White House at 10:00 p.m.

Roosevelt had entertained a black man in the White House; no other president had done that openly. By the next day, newspapers and politicians had taken the visit and twisted it with vile, racist descriptions. Other Americans defended the right of Booker T. Washington, a man who represented the cause of eleven million citizens, to be a guest in the nation's house. Washington wrote to Roosevelt later that year, noting that "the outbreak over my dining with you was far beyond my expectations" but hoping that good would come of the action. Roosevelt was hurt and made "melancholy" by the reactions of friends and foes alike. Later, he would speak with Washington publicly at events and correspond by letter, but no further invitations were issued. The *Mobile Weekly Press* published a poem in December 1901, mocking the southern outrage over the visit and defending Washington as a learned man of refinement and eloquence. The *Washington Post* detailed the following: the day of his visit to the White House, Booker T. Washington crossed paths with Austrian ambassador Hengelmuller; the men's coats were mixed up, and Hengelmuller reported that he found a rabbit's foot "killed in the dark of the moon" in Washington's pocket, a nasty snipe at the ancient traditions of black beliefs and rituals as twisted by white storytellers. The coats were sorted out, but whether there was a rabbit's foot may be only a legend—although the *Detroit News* took up in support of Washington, saying that Hengelmuller might have taken the coat but he certainly couldn't fill Washington's shoes.

The visit was famous. In contrast, almost nothing is known about Joplin's *A Guest of Honor*, and no music remains. Joplin took the completed show on the road by 1903, traveling through Iowa, Missouri, Nebraska, Kansas and Illinois with a full production (a few ads noted that there were thirty cast members, pretty girls and sweet singers). The size of the cast indicates that Joplin expanded the story well beyond the two main characters, but no reviews exist of the opera or its music. Mention is made of two song titles, however: "The Dudes Parade" and "Patriotic Patrol." Ragtime historian Edward Berlin believed that the tunes may have been published under other titles, a tantalizing mystery yet to be solved.

During the *A Guest of Honor* tour, Joplin's opera company faced serious financial difficulties, including the theft of box office receipts. The loss of funds and the limited backing for the work caused the show to shut down, and according to the lore surrounding *A Guest of Honor*, Joplin was forced to leave behind a trunk of manuscripts as collateral for a rooming house bill. Where this happened is still unknown, with guesses being made about Pittsburgh, Pennsylvania, Pittsburg, Kansas, or other places along the railroad line. No one knows whether or not Joplin went back for the trunk.

Joplin died in 1917 at age forty-nine after a long illness. His wife, Lottie, survived her husband by thirty-seven years and became the keeper of the ragtime flame, befriending young performers and supporting old friends. In 1950, Lottie was interviewed by Kay Thompson and told the following story:

When Scott died, he was composing a ragtime symphony, which he believed would be his most important effort. Unfortunately, he died before he finished it completely, and up to now, I've never mentioned it, or showed it to any writer. I felt people wouldn't understand it. Besides, they would only pester me to death. As it is, every once in a while, someone comes around, wanting to know if Scott left any "unfinished" manuscripts…One reason I don't have more than I do is that Scott destroyed a lot of things before his last illness. He was afraid that, if anything happened to him, they might get stolen.

Not long before Lottie's death, the musician Dr. John "Knocky" Parker visited her and purchased some music, although he noted that *A Guest of Honor* was not there. Then, in the mid-1960s, ragtime performer Robert Darch claimed to have located the score of *A Guest*, and Walter Hill of Sedalia later said that he had discovered several manuscript pages from *Guest*. Neither man allowed anyone to examine the finds in detail, and to this day, *Guest* remains lost.

Perhaps the manuscript was never lost but reclaimed by Joplin, who was disappointed enough over the failure of his first opera that he tossed it aside. Perhaps he destroyed the score later in life. Or perhaps there just may be a full score sitting in a Missouri attic, awaiting discovery once again. Today, Joplin is honored as a seminal figure in the development of American popular music, and his works take listeners back to a time when rags were an art. But perhaps his greatest gift was to show that music and talent are best when colorblind.

Chapter 20

Ho, Ho, MO and Holiday Legends

Among the most famous holiday films is *Miracle on 34*[th] *Street,* in which a department store Santa may or may not be the real North Pole toymaker. The film was partly set in Macy's, New York City, still a magnet for the world in the weeks between Thanksgiving and Christmas. Santa's appearance always anchors the Macy's Thanksgiving Day Parade, ushering in the holiday and shopping season with giant balloons, song, dance and a magnificent sleigh with reindeer. But right up there with Manhattan as a holiday destination stands Missouri, home to the first department store Santa this side of the Mississippi.

Herman Zuzak was born on September 12, 1876, in Louisiana, Missouri. By his early twenties, he was a businessman with a penchant for advertising and promotion who owned two buildings (311 and 313) on Main Street in Boonville. The shops were built after the Civil War and at various times sold books, clothing and general goods, but Zuzak combined the two spaces and named the emporium Zuzak's Wonder Store. Always a local booster and an imaginative entrepreneur, Zuzak realized one year that he could capitalize on the slow shopping season just after Thanksgiving by advertising a visit from St. Nick. So in 1897, an unnamed Santa Claus dressed in a red suit, donned a hat, climbed aboard a ferryboat near old Franklin and rode across the Missouri to the Boonville dock. Unlike his Christmas Eve visits, Santa was not alone, trailing along with him horses, a decorated sleigh, gifts, candy and dignitaries from the town and beyond. A crowd greeted the jolly elf at Zuzak's, and he spent the afternoon meeting children and their families and distributing toys and candy to the large crowds. The response over the years was overwhelming, with Santa having to haul in more than one thousand pounds of candy. Human Zuzak continued the tradition of offering inexpensive holiday gifts and goods and traveling far afield to do so. A *New York Times* listing of buyers notes that Zuzak was staying at the Commodore Hotel and hoped to purchase rugs, leather goods, toys and one-dollar merchandise.

No one is certain where or when the first department store Santa enchanted visitors. Some say that James Edgar of Brockton, Massachusetts, made a Santa suit and wore it for his customers in 1890; others suggested that once Thomas Nast drew his first Santa Claus in the 1860s, shop owners took advantage of the advertising magic inherent in Christmas and offered their own St. Nick, Santa or Father

Christmas. But no matter who was first back east, unless other evidence comes to light, it appears Missouri led the way for department store Santas of the West.

Herman Zuzak eventually left the retail management world behind to work as a promoter for other Missouri businesses. He remained a steadfast booster for Boonville until his death on March 12, 1942. In a wonderful twist to this tale, it should be noted that Herman Zuzak was buried in Gates of Peace, a Jewish cemetery in Louisiana, Missouri. The spirit of goodwill at Zuzak's Wonder Store may have dressed like Santa, but it embraced all people, regardless of beliefs or traditions.

ANCIENT FRANCE IN THE MISSISSIPPI VALLEY

Each New Year's Eve, two towns in the United States celebrate an ancient French custom of caroling from door to door and begging neighbors for holiday food and drink. The tradition is called, variously, La Guignolée or La Guiannée and is held in Prairie du Rocher, Illinois, which began the custom in 1722 and has continued it for nearly three centuries. In Missouri, Ste. Genevieve was the first permanent European settlement west of the Mississippi River, but the celebration of La Guignolée had all but disappeared from the memories of French descendants when it was revived, and it continues to commemorate the Mississippi River Valley French settlements.

In Ste. Genevieve, French customs and holidays are kept as in the old country, and La Guignolée was part of life. On New Year's Eve, groups of singers disguise themselves in odd costumes and travel throughout the town stopping at homes and businesses, where they sing a traditional song and beg for meat and drink with which to celebrate the New Year. The word "guignolée" translates as the "New Year mistletoe," perhaps indicating ancient Celtic celebrations. Some historians believe the tradition goes back to medieval times, when beggars were allowed to approach the wealthy at a holiday and ask for money and food to see them through the winter. Others believe the tradition is much older and is related to ancient rites of sacrifice and rebirth at the New Year. But whatever its origin, La Guignolée still includes dancing, singing and goodwill from singers and hosts.

Today, both men and women participate in La Guignolée, but in the past, the singers have traditionally been male. On New Year's Eve, singers would assemble, don their costumes of masks, old clothing, ribbons and bells and ride horseback throughout the village, stopping at the homes of the wealthy and singing a traditional song:

> *Good day master and mistress and all who dwell in this house,*
> *On this, the last day of the year, you do owe us the guignolée.*
> *If nothing you wish to give us, pray tell us so;*

171

The song of La Guignolée demands outrageous gifts of food—including a piece of meat ninety feet long—and asks that the eldest daughter join the singers for dancing and dining, with a wink and a nod at other, less innocent occupations for the evening:

> *If nothing you wish to give us, pray tell us so;*
> *Your eldest daughter instead we will bring.*
> *Well will she be fed, warm will she be kept*

But it was all in good fun, and few families were insulted. Those who opened their homes to the singers invited them in, offered refreshments and listened to or joined in the singing; those who turned away the celebrants were often reviled with a song about unfriendly misers. La Guignolée was eventually adopted in other forms by French communities, including New Orleans and parts of Cajun country, where it is sometimes connected with Mardi Gras celebrations instead of the New Year.

Lady Apples

Charles Bell was born in Germany but moved with his family to Boonville when he was six. He took part in the Civil War when only thirteen and was captured and held in the courthouse before being released once he promised not to take up arms against the Confederacy. As a young man, he was told to move west for his health, so by train, covered wagon and foot, he headed to Colorado and began an apple-selling business, connecting growers and wholesalers. He returned to Boonville in 1878, planted extensive orchards and continued to act as a supplier of apples from around Missouri. One year, Bell purchased apples from a Scotsman in Rocheport and received several barrels of tiny bright red and green apples. The grower said that the apples were from trees he had imported from Europe, and Bell passed the barrels along to his agents, thinking nothing more of the transaction. Weeks later, Bell received payment and was astonished at the price the apples had brought, as well as the demand from the agents for more "lady apples." These tiny apples, also known as pomme d'api, were an ancient hardy variety that ripened later in the year. Along with their sweet taste, the apples' colors made them a coveted fruit at the winter holidays. Only the most elegant hotels and ocean liners served the apples during the Christmas season, and the fruits were always in demand.

Bell immediately saw the possibilities for an orchard of lady apples and set about establishing one near Merna, Missouri—although not without some setbacks. Apples do not grow true to seed; if you have a perfect apple and plant six of its seeds, you will end up with six different apples and none true to the parent. Growers had learned to graft buds from the scion, or original tree, onto rootstock. This resulted in a copy of the parent tree (and fruit). So Bell began the slow grafting process. But after two years, instead of fine young trees, all of Bell's grafted trees had knots at the grafting site. Friends from the state horticultural society told Bell that the young trees were infected and must be pulled up and burned to save the rest of his orchard. Bell refused and spent days examining each of the trees. He was lucky to have followed his instincts, because he soon realized the problem: he had grafted the small lady apples onto rootstock that grew larger and faster, resulting in the harmless knots.

Bell's devotion to the lady apple paid off, and he became the largest supplier in the world, shipping railroad carloads of the apples around the globe. Bell later founded the International Apple Shippers Association in order to promote what he called the "king of fruit," and his orchards are still producing apples. He was proud of his accomplishments, and his grand home still stands in Boonville. Both the house and his grave are topped with statues of bells, although it would have been just as appropriate to depict apples.

Chapter 21

The Mysterious Pearl

The summer of 1913 in St. Louis was miserable, with the weather alternating between hot and droughty and hot and humid, both of which were unappealing in the days when a breeze and an open window might provide the only relief. One evening in July, two St. Louis housewives left their husbands playing cards and sat down to share a Ouija board. One of the women had lost her father recently and hoped to receive a message from him in the spirit world. Although a popular name for the board was Ouija (from the French and German words for "yes"), these communicators were also known as talking boards. The flat wooden board had the alphabet and numbers printed on its surface. Users placed their fingers on a planchette or pointer that rested on the board and presumably would be moved by spirits to spell out messages. The two women—Emily Grant Hutchings and Pearl Curran—were surprised when the pointer began to move quickly across the board, indicating the message: "Many moons ago I lived. Again I come. Patience Worth is my name. Wait, I would speak with thee." The women were startled, but what came next was astounding: Patience declared her friendship for Pearl and, over the next weeks, began to communicate her story to Pearl through the Ouija board.

Spiritualism had a strong base in the United States, and many people used séances, talking boards and other methods to contact the spirit world. Hutchings and Curran were not alone in their interest, but it was rare for anyone to reach beyond the veil and receive such a visit. According to Patience's messages, she was born in England in 1649 or 1694 and immigrated to America, where she died at the hands of Indians and was buried in Massachusetts. The spirit soon began to dictate poems, novels, a play and other writings through Pearl's fingers, and transcriptionists were brought in to record the texts. Very soon, Pearl realized that she did not have to write anything but could merely open her mind to Patience and then repeat what the spirit said. This literary partnership continued for nearly twenty-four years, during which time thousands of people witnessed Pearl's "channeling" of her spirited writing partner.

Both Pearl Curran and Patience Worth gained national attention, and Patience had several of her books published. Critics praised the writings, claiming that the language and syntax used were authentic and dated from the seventeenth century and that Pearl—a moderately educated housewife—would have little knowledge of the material she was channeling. Patience was interviewed on more than one occasion by journalists, professors and others, answering questions with lively jests, moral musings and witty retorts. Others, though, questioned the honesty of Pearl, claiming that she was promoting her own work through a scam. Pearl and her husband benefited little from Patience's talent. After John's death, Pearl struggled to raise their children, remarried twice and lived out her life in the shadow of a spirit, dying in 1937.

The mystery of Patience Worth remains unsolved. Many people have studied the legend and offered theories, including that Curran had a submerged personality that surfaced as Patience, that Curran and her husband were frauds or that Patience Worth actually existed on another plane. But while Patience herself is fascinating, the story behind the legend is just as intriguing, involving spirits, water lilies and Mark Twain.

Despite the general description of Pearl and John Curran as average and middle class, they in fact sat somewhat higher in St. Louis society. John was the Missouri commissioner of immigration, responsible for the registration, prosecution and deportation of aliens, and was well respected for his work. Pearl studied music as a young woman and was remembered by friends as a lively letter writer but an indifferent student. The couple was financially comfortable—at least comfortable enough to entertain the hundreds of visitors who streamed through the Curran home and watched Pearl

"work" with Patience. Later, the Currans established the Patience Worth Press to promote the novels, poems and stories "written" by Worth through Pearl Curran. A 1920 interview with John Curran noted:

> *In the six years of production of Patience Worth works,*
> *the expenses to the Currans have been $5,905.39,*
> *and the receipts from all sources, chiefly book royalties,*
> *have been $1,854.33. "In figuring the expenses,"*
> *Mr. Curran explained, "we haven't counted the cost*

of entertaining some 8,000 persons at our home. Our callers have come Monday and Thursday evenings of every week." "Nor the expense of caring for Patience Worth Wee," Mrs. Curran added. Patience Worth Wee is a little girl whom the Currans adopted and who, it has been announced, is to be brought up in accordance with directions the spirit of Patience Worth may give.

Whoever Patience Worth was—a second personality of Pearl's or a spirit—she produced writings that displayed literary skill, style and an immediacy of place and time, rare gifts for any author. (Patience herself denied that she was Pearl: "She be but she, and I be me," claimed the spirit.) Pearl also wrote a short story that was turned into a successful 1920 silent film. The plot revolved around a young woman who believed she had psychic powers, so it appears that Pearl was not trying to hide her story from a public now entranced with Patience Worth.

The more shadowy player in this legend was Emma "Emily" Grant Hutchings, born to German parents in Hannibal, Missouri, around 1869. Emily's mother was trained in medicine, which was unusual for the time, and Emily herself was as strong-minded as they come. After completing school in Missouri, she attended a German school for a year and then returned to the United States and graduated from the University of Missouri with a bachelor of letters. She worked as a librarian, lecturer and later as a journalist in St. Louis, writing under both her own name and at least seven pseudonyms, including "Frank Harwin." She eventually became known for her human interest stories. Having grown up in Hannibal, Emily was entranced by the writings of Sam Clemens and met "Mark Twain" when he visited St. Louis in 1902. She attempted to correspond with Twain, who courteously replied to her musings about writing and then noted on the letter, "Idiot. Preserve this." Twain died in 1910 and, with him, any chance for more great literature set in Missouri. At least one would think so.

Hutchings is credited with "introducing" Pearl Curran to Patience Worth, although apparently the outcome was less than she expected. Although Ouija boards were often worked by two people, in a short time Curran did not need Hutchings and went on to "talk" with Patience Worth alone. Hutchings seemed to take affront at this, claiming that she was shown the door because she wanted to subject the Patience Worth phenomenon to "scientific inquiry" and was denied the chance by the Currans.

Less than two years after Patience "appeared," Hutchings sent a sample of "her" new book to William Marion Reedy for comments. Reedy was the publisher of *Reedy's Mirror* in St. Louis. As a champion of Pearl Curran and Patience Worth, Reedy was familiar with Hutchings. Now calling herself a psychic, Hutchings finally revealed to Reedy that the book had been sent to Hutchings, psychic Lola Hayes and psychic researcher James Hervey

Hyslop by none other than Mark Twain. Hutchings claimed that at first, Patience Worth appeared to them, but soon after, Twain became the main spirit. Hyslop was a prodigious writer and researcher into the psychic, as well as a professor of ethics and philosophy. He wrote extensively about his attempts to debunk the book titled *Jap Herron*—including his belief that Twain was relieved that he could now reveal to the world that life did, indeed, continue after death. (In an ironic twist, Hyslop called Pearl Curran a fake and a con artist.)

Jap Herron tells the story of a young Missourian man who faces down adversity and becomes a newspaper editor. The book was rejected by publishing houses before Mitchell Kennerley, a New York publisher with a flair for the odd, released it. The reviews were not kind, including this from the *New York Times* on September 9, 1917: "If this is the best that Mark Twain can do by reaching across the barrier [death], the admirers that his works have won for him will all hope that he will hereafter respect that boundary." The next year, Twain's publisher, Harper & Brothers, and Twain's daughter, Clara, sued Kennerly and Hutchings to halt publication and destroy the books. The newspapers had a field day with the story, quoting from the book and pillorying the text and the authors. Many readers looked forward to the court testimony, wondering whether Twain might be called to testify and if this might settle the case for immortality. But Kennerly and Hutchings decided against continuing the battle and agreed to cease publication and destroy the remaining copies, making *Jap Herron* a rare item for the modern collector.

Hyslop died in 1920, leaving money for the treatment of personality disorders by psychic mediums. He was said to have returned and contacted mediums after his death. Emily Hutchings had a water lily named after her and continued writing novels and stories until her death in 1951. Patience Worth seems to have returned to the next world, and her daughter disappeared from public view. Today, few novels are produced by Ouija board, but it just may be that Missouri spirits are waiting for the right time.

Chapter 22

Vanishing Point

Jerrold and Carrie Potter, an insurance executive and his wife, boarded a DC-3 on June 29, 1968, for a flight from Illinois to Texas, where they were to attend a Lion's Club convention. Potter, of Pontiac, Illinois, was a successful, happy middle-aged man with no known enemies or mental aberrations. He and Carrie had raised two daughters, and he was an active member of several community organizations. His friends thought him friendly, enthusiastic and honest, and there was no reason to believe he had anything resembling a secret life or secret woes.

The plane was owned by Purdue Airlines, a subsidiary of Purdue University, and the airline was the only one in the world that trained students in the flight industry. The DC-3 was a workhorse, a dependable airplane known for its ability to land on grass or pavement and for its stability and safety. As the plane passed over the general area of Rolla, Missouri, at eight thousand feet, Jerrold got up to use the restroom. He chatted with a few acquaintances on his way down the aisle and locked himself in the tiny room. A few minutes later, passenger James Schaive felt a small bump as the plane seemed to hit an air pocket, followed by a slight rush of air. At the same time, the pilot noticed that a warning sign was blinking that meant that a door was ajar. (The pilot, Miguel Raul Cabeza, had his own harrowing story to tell. In 1958, he was a pilot for a Cuban airline when Castro took power. Cabeza was kidnapped from a Cuban airport and forced at gunpoint to fly a planeload of refugees fleeing Havana to New York. He settled in the United States and began his flight career.) As the co-pilot, Roy Bacus, went to check, Carrie became concerned about Jerrold's absence and requested assistance from a stewardess, asking her to check on Jerrold. Bacus and the stewardess quickly discovered that the restroom was empty and the rear exit door was slightly ajar. A safety chain used to secure the plane exit door was on the floor. A thorough search of the plane was made, and the pilot headed to Springfield, Missouri, for an emergency landing. The plane's flight path was searched, but Jerrold Potter had disappeared somewhere into the skies above Missouri. Upon landing, the plane was impounded by the National Transportation Safety Board.

The Potter vanishing continues to be one of the unsolved mysteries of American aviation. The legend is constantly debated on paranormal websites. No one heard or saw anyone near the door, which had clear warning signage. If Potter had become ill and staggered to the door or even leaned against it, the door handle was almost impossible to turn without assistance, especially when the plane was in flight. Cabins of DC-3s were unpressurized (they had been used for air cargo and parachute drops), meaning that you had to stand in the door to exit, and the effort to push open the door would have flooded the plane with air and noise. Newspapers repeated the story, yet some facts were left out. The *New York Times* and other papers, in fact, reported that "the door flew open." "Nobody knows what happened," said Jim Schaive of Ottawa, Illinois. "It just suddenly happened. There was a loud noise, the plane sort of quivered a little bit and the door came open…Three men said they heard a 'swoosh' and thought something must be wrong, but didn't see anything."

From the "slight bump" of the traditional description to the "loud noise" and "the door came open" of the news articles, the stories were inconsistent, indicating, perhaps, a freak accident with tragic, if spooky, results. Five days after Potter's disappearance, his widow filed an $800,000 lawsuit against Purdue Airlines. His body was never found, and an official explanation was never provided for the disappearance.

Selected Bibliography

Legends appear in the most unlikely of places and often take much unraveling before one can knit together the strands of a story. The sources below provided background information for some of the legends in this book.

Colt, Miriam Davis. *Went to Kansas*. Watertown, NY: L. Ingalls & Co., 1862.

Douglass, Robert Sidney. *History of Southeast Missouri*. Chicago: Lewis Publishing Company, 1912.

Edmunds, David R. *The Shawnee Prophet*. Lincoln: University of Nebraska Press, 1983.

Evans, Kevin R., and John R. Bertalott. "Geology of the War of 1812: Terrain Influences on the Battle of Cote Sans Dessein, Missouri Territory." *Geological Society of America Abstracts* 43, no. 1 (2011): 100.

Hermance, J. Noel. *William Wells Brown and Clotelle*. N.p.: Archon Books, 1969.

Missouri Division, United Daughters of the Confederacy. *Reminiscences of the Women of Missouri During the Sixties*. Jefferson City, MO: Hugh Stephens Printing Company, n.d.

Randolph, Vance. *Ozark Superstitions*. New York: Columbia University Press, 1947.

Stewart, Watson. *Personal Memoirs of Watson Stewart*. 1904. www.kancoll.org/articles/stewart/ws_section01.htm.

Thomas, John L. *Missouri Historical Review* 2, no. 1 (October 1907).

Wetmore, Alphonso. *Gazetteer of the State of Missouri*. St. Louis, MO: Charles Keemle, 1837.

Williams, Walter, ed. *A History of Northeast Missouri*. Chicago: Lewis Publishing, 1913.

Newspapers
Columbia Missourian
Missouri Intelligencer and Boonslick Advertiser
Missouri Republican

About the Author

Mary Barile was born in New York City and raised on Long Island. She studied music and literature at Hofstra University and was a member of the Long Island Symphony. She moved to Missouri in 2001 and is currently associate director of grants for the University of Missouri, where she teaches grant writing. She received her PhD from Mizzou in theater history. Mary is the author of several books on popular culture and travel and a published playwright. Her plays have been performed in the United States and Canada, and she is the scriptwriter for a documentary film about actress Maude Adams. Among her research interests are Missouri history, ghosts and legends. Mary is a board member of the Missouri Parks Association and the Baa Baa Boonville Rug Hookers, a devoted group of wool artists. She lives in Boonville, where she steps out into history each morning.

VISIT US AT
WWW.HISTORYPRESS.NET